DR KEVIN

CHRISTIANITY IS GOOD FOR US

Why Faith Matters

FOREWORD BY CARDINAL GEORGE PELL

Published by:
Wilkinson Publishing Pty Ltd
ACN 006 042 173

PO Box 24135, Melbourne, Victoria, Australia 3001
Ph: 03 9654 5446
www.wilkinsonpublishing.com.au

Copyright © 2021 Dr Kevin Donnelly

A catalogue record for this book is available from the National Library of Australia

ISBN(s): 9781925927795: Paperback

Design by Spike Creative Pty Ltd
Ph: (03) 9427 9500
spikecreative.com.au

Printed and bound in Australia by Griffin Press, part of Ovato

WilkinsonPublishing

wilkinsonpublishinghouse

WPBooks

The central role of Christianity in our national culture is clearly under attack. Such struggles require committed warriors. Through his collection of articles and columns, Kevin has proved himself to be a great warrior.

John Howard, former prime minister of Australia

On our current discontents, there is no more thoughtful, better informed and prolific writer than Kevin Donnelly. Here is nearly all you need to know about the centrality of Christianity to our culture; why and how it's in eclipse; and what should be done to make a bad situation better; all delivered in easy-to-read, self-contained essays that the mind can easily absorb. Well said — and thank you!

Tony Abbott, former prime minister of Australia

Australian society is in the midst of significant cultural change. The Christian underpinnings of our society are being steadily and systematically removed. There is a determined and aggressive campaign being waged to eliminate the presence and contribution of Christianity to the Australian way of life. Voices need to be raised to alert the many people of good will to what is happening around them. Kevin Donnelly has been one such voice. This collection of articles written for newspapers and magazines have sought to reach out to the general public. There is a place for the academic paper, but now, more than ever, there is a need for a voice in the public square. Kevin has a special skill in articulating what is happening in the culture. I recommend this book as a source of insight into what is the battle for the future of our Australian way of life.

Julian Porteous, Catholic Archbishop of Hobart

In this collection of articles Kevin Donnelly explains the superiority of virtues over values, explains the Church schools' contribution to increasing social capital, reinforcing societal glue, strengthening the community fabric; their consistently superior academic and employment results and the financial contribution of parents over nearly 150 years to both capital and running costs. The public needs to be reminded of these basic truths.

Cardinal George Pell

Kevin Donnelly cites author and atheist Douglas Murray in this thoughtful and important selection of essays. Murray argues that 'to appreciate Western culture is to recognise the importance of Christianity'. You won't agree with everything Donnelly writes in these essays championing Christianity — I don't — but it is impossible not to emerge from reading these pieces without feeling cheered and reassured by the way Judeo-Christian faith and principles have underpinned the creation and maintenance of Western civilisation. Impossible also not to feel chilled, given the precedents of Stalin's Russia, Mao's China and Hitler's Germany, by what happens when societies — and their children — are forced to reject such faith.

Shelley Gare, Journalist and commentator

Kevin Donnelly succeeds, where others have faltered, in making a powerful case why faith matters, especially Christianity. Through a variety of publications, on a wide range of subjects, he has demonstrated why Christian faith is a cornerstone of much that is good in our national life. Dr Donnelly is generous-spirited and good hearted, but never woke or politically correct. His views, therefore, are refreshing and enlightening.

Tess Livingstone, Journalist at The Australian and author

Dr Kevin Donnelly AM has brought together a valuable collection of his writings on faith and culture. His writings shine a light on the fundamental importance of Christianity in modern Australia even as it faces attack by belligerent anti-religious secularists. In this volume, Kevin astutely documents many facets of the increasing hostility to Christianity. Through all his writings, Kevin presents a thoughtful, winsome and persuasive explanation of the central importance of Christianity to a richer and fuller and flourishing Australian society. In the tradition of Augustine, readers should tolle lege — take up and read — this excellent book.

John Steenhof, Principal Lawyer, Human Rights Law Alliance

Kevin Donnelly is a battle-hardened warrior in the campaign to protect Australia from the crazy follies of the radical left. He knows a naked emperor when he sees one and he'll fearlessly call him out. He's not concerned to promote particular doctrines, but he does insist that modern Australia was founded as a Christian country, that Christian morality permeates our inherited laws and customs, and that we are fools or worse if we lightly cast these things aside.

David Daintree, Christopher Dawson Centre

What a superb antidote to cultural amnesia and political correctness! Kevin Donnelly's wide-ranging, perceptive compendium of articles reminds us all that Western civilisation's art, music, literature and political legacy can only be understood in its spiritual context. A must-read for students of history and culture!

Wanda Skowronska, Educational psychologist and author

Liberal democracies, with their sense of 'separation' (if also regular collaboration) between Church and State, are an inheritance from Christianity. So is so much else we value in our culture and polity, as Kevin Donnelly demonstrates. Yet we increasingly find ourselves in a society that has forgotten how to reason, propose, listen, dialogue, learn from each other. Instead we encounter tribal prejudice, ideological slogans, manufactured indignation, cancel culture and the rest, which make the culture inhospitable not only to faith but also to reason, and so to liberalism itself. As Pope Francis has pointed out, we can only hope to make things better by evangelising the culture; and we can only hope to do that effectively by understanding where it is and why and what can be done about it, and by starting first with ourselves, improving the quality of our own conversation. Christianity is Good For Us meets both these charges, giving the writer's impressions as to where we've come from, presently stand and are tending, and offering a thoughtful if often provocative response. Highly recommended!

Archbishop Fisher

Contents

Foreword

Recently some lesser lights and indeed some brighter lights of the anti-Christian movement have proclaimed that Christian voices should no longer be given a hearing in public discussion. It is as though Christian churches, schools, hospitals, and retirement homes will continue to be seen (no name changes necessary yet), but their voices will not be heard.

This clumsy bluff is, of course, quite ineffective, even when it is backed by waves of social media abuse, while writers such as Kevin Donnelly continue to publish their thoughts, positive, reasonable, and courteous contributions. Kevin contributes broadly on many topics, ranging from COVID-19 to heteronormativity, from China to Catholic schools to Islam. He is not reluctant to repeat his message, being well aware of that basic principle of learning that most people will not remember a point until they have heard it two or three times. However, the articles are grouped around three themes: the centrality of Judeo-Christianity to Western Civilisation, the importance of faith-based schools and freedom of religion under attack.

The author has a multiplicity of riches to be mined in our new world. A recent high point was reached whereby resources available to schools suggest any young boy or young girl, who is not allowed to vote or drive a car and forbidden to buy alcohol or cigarettes, is now able to commence changing his or her sex without the permission of their parents. It is not a thought crime to suspect this is from *Alice in Wonderland*, but it is illegal to try to dissuade the child from such a choice, especially if prayers were to be used. Probably the legislators on these issues wept at their success, like Alexander the Great lamenting that he had no worlds left to conquer.

Theirs is a legacy which will be remembered.

China had not ventured far in its hostile rhetoric and punitive trade measures, and neither had the COVID-19 plague ravaged most of the world when these articles were being written. Even then, important changes had been occurring in Australia, unrecognised by many of the population.

Most of the arts and humanities faculties in our universities have been conquered by a reactionary left-wing wave, which is not only hostile to Christianity, but to the Western culture which has produced Europe, the United States, and Australia (merely a start to the list), and which includes the Renaissance, the Enlightenment, modern science, and the French and American Revolutions. We are confronting a heady brew of Marx and Woodstock, often further poisoned by the anonymous 'pile-ons' of the social media.

About thirteen Confucius Institutes have been created in Australian universities, without controversy, for the study of Chinese culture and courses have been introduced for the study of Islam. Both China and Islam are ancient, mighty, and different civilisations, which need to be studied by us.

What is strange and revealing is that when the Ramsay Institute offered to finance three courses on Western civilisation in Australian universities, ferocious public opposition erupted, often from academic staff. It was as though one might peacefully study almost any topic, provided it was not our story, not the study of our magnificent achievements as prosperous, free, and modern democracies and our tragic failures, and provided you were hostile and disparaging of our history.

When universities are largely funded by taxpayers, government has a right to demand that our Australian history, rooted in Europe, our institutions, and our thought world have a prominent place in the curriculum for sympathetic study and critical evaluation. Donnelly has done sterling work in bringing these issues into the light.

Faith-based non-government schools are another of Donnelly's central concerns and a major factor in Australian public life where they educate around 34 per cent of all students. Immediate pressure points are the rights of such schools to control their staff appointments and enrolments. Both rights are vital and must be defended publicly and politically. Just as all political parties have a right to reject work applicants for their organisations who do not share their vision, so do schools, hospitals, and other religious institutions. If I applied to work for the Communists or the Greens, they would be entitled to reject my application, not simply because of my longevity, but because I would work in their employ to damage their interests.

Donnelly explains the superiority of virtues over values, explains the Church schools' contribution to increasing social capital, reinforcing societal glue, strengthening the community fabric; their consistently superior academic and employment results and the financial contribution of parents over nearly 150 years to both capital and running costs. The public needs to be reminded of these basic truths.

There is only one example of unanimity in the New Testament when the Gerasene swine, all possessed by demons charged over the cliff to drown in the Sea of Galilee. True democracies value free speech, diversity of opinion, genuine tolerance, the vigorous but courteous discussion and debate necessary to maintain what we have achieved and build further.

Kevin Donnelly is playing a vital role in our national life by his sometimes provocative, but always cogent and respectful views and arguments. Long may he flourish.

George Cardinal Pell

11 May 2021

Introduction

Ignored by those attacking Christianity and seeking to bring about a neo-Marxist inspired utopia is that Christianity is one of the foundation stones of Western civilisation and liberal democracies like Australia and, on balance, its strengths and benefits far outweigh its sins.

As noted by T. S. Eliot in *Notes towards a Definition of Culture* 'To our Christian heritage we owe many things beside religious faith. Through it we trace the evolution of our arts, through it we have our conception of Roman Law which has done so much to shape the Western world, through it we have our conceptions of private and public morality'.

Concepts like the inherent dignity of the person, the right to liberty and freedom and a commitment to social justice and the common good arose as a result of Christ's teachings detailed in the New Testament. The preamble to Australia's Constitution contains the words 'Humbly relying on the blessing of Almighty God' and parliaments around Australia begin with the Lord's Prayer.

The evolution of Australia's legal system, initially drawing on William Blackstone's *Commentaries on the Laws of England* and the importance of British common law, is also underpinned by Christianity proven by the practice of swearing on the Bible and the overriding belief one's responsibility is to do good instead of harm.

Much of Western civilisation's art, music and literature can only be understood and appreciated in the context of Christianity and the life of Jesus. It's no accident that much of the West's literary canon deals with religious concepts like good and evil, temptation and betrayal, atonement and redemption and a thirst for moral certainty and spiritual fulfilment.

Christianity, especially the Catholic Church, plays a significant role in health, education, welfare and much needed charitable and social welfare services that in addition to serving the common good and promoting social cohesion and reciprocity save governments and taxpayers billions of dollars every year. In relation to education, for example, Australian Catholic schools enrol approximately 20% of students, saving the impost if such students attended government schools.

In an increasingly materialistic, ego driven world devoid of spiritual succour and transcendence Christianity also provides a rich and potent source of nourishment that provides reassurance, comfort and the belief as stated by the Christian mystic Julian of Norwich that 'And all shall be well. And all shall be well. And all manner of things shall be well.'

Proven by Pope John Paul II's vehement opposition to communism and his role in eventually freeing Poland from a godless, totalitarian regime, one of the greatest strengths of Christianity is that it provides a bulwark against dictatorships. As detailed by the Italian philosopher Augusto Del Noce in *The Crisis of Modernity*, the concept of original sin, free will and the belief this worldly life is ephemeral works against ideologies promising a paradise on Earth. No matter how much communism promises the workers' paradise those who know the Bible understand the dangers of worshiping demagogues and believing in a man-made utopia.

Despite Christianity's invaluable contribution and vital importance, there's no doubt in Western nations like Australia it's a hard time being a Christian, especially a Catholic. Since the time Jesus walked with his disciples and was crucified Christianity has suffered periods of great hostility, deprivation and abuse but such is the unique and all-encompassing nature of recent and ongoing attacks that some commentators fear we are now living in a godless, post-Christian age.

In the public domain and in many people's minds Catholicism is immediately associated with the evil crime of paedophilia and the fact for far too long innocent and vulnerable children were made to suffer. Such is the pain and lost innocence of those abused that understandably many feel disappointment and anger and any mention of religion elicits a negative and hostile response.

Such is the materialistic and ego-centred nature of Western societies it's also the case that instead of valuing and committing to a transcendent and spiritual sense of life many define themselves in terms of what they can achieve and possess in the here and now. Individuals no longer acknowledge or give themselves up to a higher and more sublime sense of this world and the life to come.

As argued by Del Noce, those committed to a scientific and technocratic view of the world also consider religion to be unnecessary and irrelevant. The world and the cosmos are not God ordained and humanity has the power to control nature and to shape its own destiny. Man has the power to split the atom, put a man on the moon, conduct open heart surgery and fertilise an egg outside the womb via invitro fertilisation.

The rise of neo-Marxism and critical theory initially associated with Germany's Frankfurt School (established in the 1920s) represent another threat to Christianity as its adherents espouse an extreme secular view of human nature, how history evolves and how society should be structured. While classical Marxism centres on economics and the workers' struggle against capitalism neo-Marxism focuses on the Left's long march through the institutions and the culture wars.

Drawing on the concept of critical theory, Antonio's Gramsci's *The Prison Notebooks* and the speeches of the German student radical Rudi Dutschke the strategy adopted, instead of taking to the streets and storming the barricades, involves infiltrating and taking control of institutions like schools, universities, the media, political parties, intermediary organisations and the church.

Since the cultural revolution of the late '60s and early '70s neo-Marxism has morphed into a rainbow alliance of radical, centre-left theories, including: postmodernism, deconstructionism, feminism and gender, queer and postcolonial narratives and tropes. While often in disagreement what all hold in common is an intense dislike and opposition to Judeo-Christianity and the teachings of the Catholic Church.

The postmodernist argument that texts have no inherent or commonly agreed meaning strikes at the very heart of Christianity as, if true, the Bible instead of espousing the word of God is simply a social construct enforcing the hegemony of the ruling class. The belief there are no absolutes and that all cultures are of equal value and worth also leads to moral relativism.

As argued by Pope Benedict XVI 'We are building a dictatorship of relativism that does not recognise anything as definitive and whose ultimate goal consists solely of one's own ego and desires'. The '60s sexual revolution, drawing on Wilhelm Reich's *The Sexual Revolution*, best illustrates the extent to which Western societies now embrace a view of human nature and sexuality in opposition to what the Bible teaches.

Such is the prevalence and force of what Sydney's Archbishop Fisher describes as a 'absolutist secularism' that anyone daring to enter the public square and defend or argue from a Christian perspective is attacked and vilified as a God botherer. Especially when dealing with controversial and sensitive issues like same-sex marriage, euthanasia, abortion and transgenderism the argument is religion must remain a private affair and there is no room in the public debate for Christian morals and beliefs.

As a result of hostility towards Christianity, Australia's tennis great Margaret Court and rugby's Israel Folau are vilified and abused for daring to oppose same-sex marriage and homosexuality. Other examples include former prime minister Tony Abbott being condemned as the mad monk and Tasmania's Archbishop Porteous taken before the anti-discrimination commission for espousing the Church's views about marriage.

The most egregious example of hostility and vindictive behaviour against a Christian involves the widespread media prejudice and bias against Cardinal George Pell during the long and exhausting legal process that led to his initial conviction and then eventual freedom as a result of the High Court's 7 to 0 decision signifying his innocence.

There's no doubt religion is far from perfect and many sins have been committed in the name of Christianity. At the same time, it's vital to acknowledge and celebrate the positive and beneficial contribution and role Christianity has played and continues to play across the globe and in nations like Australia. T.S. Eliot argues 'no culture has appeared or developed except together with a religion'. The English poet also suggests such is the inexorably interwoven nature of religion and culture that 'if Christianity goes, the whole of our culture goes'.

Christianity is Central to Western Civilisation

The power of prayer isn't lost in the modern age

The Drum
16 October 2014

The expression 'there are no atheists in the trenches', while self-serving and somewhat disingenuous, is perfectly understandable.

During moments of extreme danger, fear and the imminent risk of death, even those who don't believe in a god or the afterlife might be tempted to make an each-way bet.

It's also true that in moments of despair, sorrow and grief, after losing a loved one or after experiencing personal suffering and pain, human nature is such that we look to some deeper cause or higher explanation to assuage the sense of loss and to give some meaning to events.

For me, as I detail in my book *Taming The Black Dog*, losing a son in a hit-and-run accident triggered such a response. Why did it happen? Why is life so unexpected and cruel? And why are such random and wanton acts allowed to occur and to steal the life of somebody so full of vitality and life?

At university I studied the English mystic and poet William Blake, and one of his aphorisms suddenly came to mind: 'He who sees the infinite in all things sees God. He who sees the Ratio only, sees himself only.'

While critical of established religion, best illustrated by the poem 'Garden of Love', Blake is referring to a transcendent sense of reality and a sense of mystery very much opposed to scientific rationalism.

Our perception of the world and our place in it, by necessity, is limited and fallible, and as acknowledged by Blake, to achieve a fuller, richer and more sublime sense of self, we need to cleanse the doors of perception.

Exemplified by the world's great religions and belief systems, especially Buddhism, Christianity and Hinduism, the belief is that this materialistic, self-centred and ego-driven sense of worldly existence masks a far more profound, eternal and complete sense of reality.

And, whether chanting, singing hymns, reciting scripture or simply reflecting and meditating, it's also true that prayer is central to religion and the ability to find respite from suffering, depression and pain.

Many of the baby boomers I went to university with, following the example of the Beatles and the Maharishi Mahesh Yogi, discovered transcendental meditation while others joined rural communes and prayed to the earth goddess Gaia.

Even today, whenever friends and neighbours arrive back from Europe, they talk about vast cathedrals like Chartres, Notre Dame or St Paul's Cathedral in London; quiet, reflective places of worship and prayer away from the busy, congested streets and noisy, crowded metropolis.

As noted by Deepak Chopra, it is also the case that even atheists and agnostics can find some benefit in prayer. He writes: 'In a sceptical age, it has taken brain scans and stress research to confirm that prayer and meditation are real. There is no doubt that both are useful, with observable physiological effects. On that basis alone, they can bring the benefit of inner calm and homeostasis, and most probably aid in the healing response, without needing belief'.

Such benefits help explain the surge in wellness and stillness classes in primary schools where children raised on plasma TVs and computer games and consumed by intrusive and ever-present social networking sites are taught to find inner calm and a sense of peace.

As a Catholic, it was only natural that I turned to prayer in the hope of finding some solace and comfort and a sense that all was not lost after losing a son. Prayer signifies a sense of giving oneself up to something higher and acknowledging that to be mortal is to experience suffering and pain.

As stated by the English mystic Julian of Norwich: 'Prayer is a new, gracious, lasting will of the soul united and fast-bound to the will of God by the precious and mysterious working of the Holy Ghost'.

Prayer, in its simplest form, is also a remedy for hubris and being narcissistic. A much-needed tonic in a society where celebrity culture rules, ambition and ego prevail and the ability to find solace and calm is increasingly lost.

Christianity is the cornerstone of democratic values

The Australian
18 April 2015

In his Easter message the British Prime Minister, David Cameron, argues Britain is a Christian country and that 'The Church is not just a collection of beautiful old buildings. It is a living, active force across our country'.

Given the impact of Islamic terrorism and last year's Trojan Horse affair, where a number of Muslim schools in Birmingham were considered in danger of advocating extreme Islamic values, David Cameron also argues that all schools must teach what it means to be British.

Cameron describes British values as 'freedom, tolerance, respect for the rule of law, belief in personal and social responsibility and respect for British institutions. Those are the sorts of things I would hope would be inculcated into the curriculum in any school in Britain'.

The argument that Christianity is central to British culture, especially its political and legal systems is also, and not unexpectedly, argued by 22 Christian leaders in a document titled 'Values: The characteristics of our British national identity'.

Similar to Cameron, the Values document lists liberal, democratic values such as the rule of law, the sanctity of human life, a commitment to the common good and 'freedom of speech, debate, conscience and religion'. The argument is also put that such values are 'derived from our Judeo-Christian foundations' and 'fundamental to the health of our national life'.

Cameron, as is the German Chancellor Angela Merkel, is also on record warning that multiculturalism has failed as a government policy and that the alternative must be 'muscular liberalism'.

If young Islamic youth are not taught clear and firm values about what it means to be British and why such a way of life is worth defending then Cameron argues it shouldn't surprise if they are attracted to 'extremist ideology'.

Given Australia's political and legal systems are inherited from Britain and the fact we were settled as a British colony, it should not surprise that liberal, democratic values and Christianity are also central to our way of life.

As detailed by Murdoch University's Augusto Zimmermann, Christianity plays a major and significant role in the history of common law. In an essay titled 'A Law above the Law: Christian Roots of the English Common Law' Zimmermann argues that common law 'has an incredibly rich Christian heritage'.

He goes on to observe that 'England's most celebrated jurists – including the likes of Blackstone, Coke, and Fortescue — often drew heavily from their Christian faith when expounding and developing what are now well-established principles and doctrines'.

While the figure is now approximately 52% at Federation some 90% of Australians professed the Christian faith. Our parliaments begin with the Lord's Prayer and the Constitution's preamble includes the words 'Almighty God'.

As shown by the national day of mourning in response to the tragedy involving flight MH17 being shot down over Ukraine, with the loss of 38 Australians, it is still customary to turn to religion, especially Christianity, to help deal with unbearable loss, grief and pain.

Similar to Britain it is also true that Christian organisations like the Salvation Army, the Brotherhood of St Laurence, the St Vincent de Paul

Society and Caritas Australia work tirelessly to alleviate poverty and suffering both here and overseas.

Catholic schools enrol 20% of students around Australia, saving taxpayers and governments millions of dollars, and if Christian hospitals and aged care facilities did not exist then Australia's health and welfare systems would collapse.

Democratic concepts associated with Westminster parliamentary systems like one-person-one vote, separation of powers, governments being formed in the people's house and free and open elections evolved over some hundreds of years and ensure our freedom and liberty.

Legal concepts like innocent until proven guilty, the right to a free and timely trial, habeas corpus and the right to be judged by one's peers are also distinctive. Such rights are denied in totalitarian regimes.

Leading to a situation, as noted by the English judge Lord Denning, where 'The rulers are not under God and the Law. They are a law unto themselves. All law, all courts are simply part of the state machine. The freedom of the individual, as we know it, no longer exists'.

And the reality is millions across the world in Africa, South America, the Middle East, Indo-China and the old USSR are denied the rights we take for granted. It is also true that extreme interpretations of Islam are hostile to democratic beliefs and values.

As noted by the US based Freedom House, countries like Saudi Arabia, Syria and Iran are oppressive regimes where women, in particular, are denied basic rights and the freedom to be independent.

The barbaric and evil acts committed by the Islamic State in the name of religion, such as beheading 21 Christians, also provides a chilling example of what happens when individuals and groups turn their backs on civilised values.

In the same way that 22 Christian leaders are arguing that Judeo-Christianity is central to British identity there are also Australian religious organisations arguing, in the context of the 2014 review of the Australian national curriculum, that religion is central to our way of life.

The Catholic Education Commission of Victoria's submission argues that Judeo-Christian beliefs and values are 'the foundations of our liberal democracy'. The Anglican Education Commission argues 'Our justice, government, education, health and general welfare systems are all established on the Judeo-Christian foundation of this civilization'.

Another submission received with 1,647 signatures argues that students in government and non-government schools should learn about Christianity 'in a way that is fair and balanced'.

Those critical of Judeo-Christianity often argue that Australia is a secular society as the Constitution states that the Commonwealth 'shall not make any law for establishing any religion, or for imposing any religious observance'. While true, such a statement does not mean that religion should be banished from the public square or ignored by the curriculum.

To attempt to do so not only misinterprets the Constitution, it also weakens and undermines the very liberal, democratic institutions and values that ensure Australia, compared to many countries overseas, is such a peaceful, prosperous and just society.

Worst still, by denying this country has a strong and viable narrative worth advocating and protecting, as suggested by David Cameron, we vacate the field and allow extremist and violent ideologies to influence our young.

Pope Francis' moral message on Dante holds true for other classics

The Australian
9 May 2015

Pope Francis, on the occasion of the 750th celebration of Dante Alighieri's birthday, is in no doubt about the enduring value and significance of the *Divine Comedy*.

Even though the narrative poem, depicting Dante's allegorical journey through hell, purgatory and heaven, was written centuries ago Pope Francis believes it still resonates in today's world.

The Pope writes that Dante 'still has much to say and to offer through his immortal works to those who wish to follow the route of true knowledge and authentic discovery of self, the world and the profound and transcendent meaning of existence'.

In today's world of 30-second sound grabs, narcissistic social networking sites, texting and the need for immediate gratification talk about 'true knowledge' and 'transcendent meaning' might appear irrelevant but there is no denying that to be human is to seek such understanding.

As Milton portrays in *Essays on Man* to be human is to be incomplete as we are 'created half to rise and half to fall; Great lord of all things, yet prey to all, Sole judge of truth, in endless error hurl'd; The glory, jest and riddle of the world'.

Given such a situation it is only natural that through the arts, literature in particular, we seek to find some solace and meaning in what is a flawed and imperfect world.

Pope Francis goes on to say that the *Divine Comedy* depicts 'a true pilgrimage, both personal and intimate as well as collective, ecclesial, social and historical. It is the paradigm of every authentic journey in which humanity is called to leave behind what Dante calls 'the flowerbed that makes us so ferocious' and reach a new condition marked by harmony, peace and happiness'.

Dante's pilgrimage involves what Robin Kirkpatrick describes as an 'intellectual and spiritual struggle' exploring the 'psychology, actions and the fate of the human individual'. In particular, Dante explores human nature and actions within a Christian ethos where free will prevails and good and evil struggle for supremacy.

While concepts like sin, avarice, hubris, forgiveness, redemption, mercy and goodness might seem foreign to those steeped in a daily culture of American and Australian sitcoms and virtual chat rooms the narrative surrounding the executions of Andrew Chan and Myuran Sukumaran demonstrates that such traits and emotions are still central to our way of life.

Dante's *Divine Comedy*, as do other enduring classics like Bunyan's *Pilgrim's Progress* and more recent literary texts like C. S. Lewis' *The Chronicles of Narnia*, deal with existential questions and dilemmas about what constitutes right action and how we should relate to one another and the wider world.

Similar to Bunyan's *A Pilgrim's Progress* Dante's poem also shows how the path to goodness and understanding is often a tortuous one where temptation and weakness cause indecision, suffering and pain.

While a rainbow alliance of critical theories, ranging from neo-Marxism, feminism, queer theory, post-colonialism and post-modernism seek to deconstruct texts in terms of class, gender, power and sexuality the reality is that literature, especially the classics, are inherently moral in character.

Macbeth and Lady Macbeth suffer guilt and remorse and eventual madness and death as a result of committing regicide.

Frodo Baggins in *The Lord of the Rings* suffers as a result of being torn between keeping the ring for himself and giving up what is most precious in order to save his companions and destroy the evil Sauron.

Classic literature like the *Odyssey*, the *Iliad* and Old English tales like *Beowulf* also deal with overcoming adversity and what appear to be insurmountable challenges. Bravery, endurance and being inventive and resourceful are traits that allow the hero to succeed.

Such is the power of such tales that Hollywood regularly produces movies like *Thor* and *Troy* and TV series like *The Odyssey* and *Helen of Troy*. As noted by Joseph Campbell, the American mythologist, such tales also form the basis for modern popular classics like the *Star Wars* series of films by George Lucas.

Those familiar with Greek tragedies like *The Bacchae*, *Oedipus* and *Medea* will appreciate that human nature has not changed over thousands of years and that there is nothing unique about the emotional and psychological problems we face in our day to day lives.

At a time when many young people, given the increasing rates of self-harm, suicide and depression, appear to lack a moral compass and a sense of resilience and being grounded it is vital that they be allowed to encounter such tales.

The American academic and author of *The Closing of the American Mind*, Allan Bloom, describes how great works like those of Homer, Dante, Racine and Moliere, Goethe and Shakespeare provide a 'common understanding of what is virtuous and vicious, noble and base' to their respective cultures.

Without such works, Bloom argues, societies become atomised as there is no longer a common understanding and respect for those values and beliefs that are most worth cultivating and protecting.

Pope Francis, when applauding the *Divine Comedy*, suggests that one of its strengths is that it provides a transcendent view of life. As with all great literature there is a sense that this physical world is a veil of illusion and that our time here is finite.

To acknowledge such is the case should not be cause for despair; rather to embrace the transitory nature of life and our imperfectability is to achieve what T. S. Eliot refers to in the *Wasteland* as the 'peace which passeth understanding'.

Christianity is central to Western values and culture

The Australian
30 May 2015

As noted by the American academic Samuel P. Huntington some 10 years ago, the 'great divisions among humankind and the dominating source of conflict will be cultural'. One only needs to note the ongoing conflict between extremist versions of Islam and Western culture to see the truth of Huntington's observation.

Given the prevalence of what Huntington describes as 'the clash of civilisations' the question that must be addressed is: what makes Western civilisation unique and what aspects of our culture are most worth defending?

One response argues that there is nothing unique or special about Western culture. Those committed to multiculturalism and diversity and difference suggest Western culture is made up of various influences and traditions.

Australia, for example and since 1788, has embraced immigrants from around the world; each with their own customs, habits, beliefs and way of life that are acknowledged and celebrated.

In its more extreme form those advocating multiculturalism adopt a relativistic stance where all cultures are considered of equal worth and those seeking to champion Western civilisation are criticised for being Eurocentric, binary, patriarchal, elitist and reactionary.

During the cultural revolution of the late '60s and early '70s the radical cry on many campuses across America was 'hey, hey, ho, ho, Western Civ has got to go'. The result, as detailed in Allan Bloom's *The Closing of the American Mind*, is the death of rigorous and balanced academic studies in the liberal-humanist tradition.

As argued by La Trobe University's John Carroll in the May edition of *Quadrant*, the cultural-left's view of Western culture is one where 'art has to be shocking; values have to be deconstructed; meanings have to be exposed as rationalisations for entrenched privilege and wealth'.

A second response, as detailed by Pierre Ryckmans in his 1996 Boyer lectures, is to argue while particular cultures might be variegated it is important to recognise cultures also have unique and distinctive characteristics.

Ryckmans argues that cultures are 'indivisible' and that it is impossible to understand a foreign culture from a Western perspective 'if you do not have a firm grasp of your own'. In relation to teaching about China Ryckmans asks 'How can you explain the influence of Nietzsche upon Lu Xun to students who have never read Nietzsche?'.

T.S. Eliot in *Notes Towards a Definition of Culture* also argues while Western culture has drawn on a range of other influences there are 'common features' that identify the many nations that are heirs to the Western tradition. And central to Western culture is Christianity.

Eliot writes 'To our Christian heritage we owe many things beside religious faith. Through it we trace the evolution of our arts, through it we have our conception of Roman Law which has done so much to shape the Western world, through it we have our conceptions of private and public morality'.

While there is no doubt that philosophy, reason and the scientific method of testing truth claims traced to the Enlightenment and back further to ancient Greece have had a profound impact on Western culture it is equally true that Judeo-Christianity has had a significant and enduring influence.

As argued by the American academic Thomas E. Woods, 'Western civilization stands indebted to the Church for the university system, charitable work, international law, the sciences, important legal principles and much else besides.'

The fact that Western cultures still celebrate Christmas and Easter and that aphorisms like 'turn the other cheek', 'let he among you without sin cast the first stone' and 'render unto Caesar what is Caesar's' are still in use illustrate the impact of Christianity.

Biblical commandments like 'thou shalt not kill', 'do not steal', 'do not bear false witness' and 'do not commit adultery' underpin much of the Western legal system, as do concepts like the sanctity of life and the importance of absolution and redemption.

As noted by Augusto Zimmermann from Murdoch University, 'The common law was heavily influenced by Christian philosophy. This philosophy argues that there is a divine reason for the existence of fundamental laws, and that such laws are superior to human-made legislation'.

The evil nature of totalitarian regimes like communism and fascism is that they are premised on the belief that man made laws reign supreme, that power and violence instead of reason are the final arbiters and that utopia can be created on this earth.

While secular critics argue that faith and reason are antithetical to one another is also true that Christian scholars and intellectuals have contributed in a significant way to Western culture's intellectual heritage.

Central to Cardinal Newman's concept of a university is the formation of a habit of mind 'which lasts through life, of which the attributes are freedom, equitableness, calmness, moderation and wisdom'. Although written over 150 years ago what Newman argues provides a healthy tonic to those who view education as simply about promoting productivity and economic competitiveness.

Christian philosophers like St Thomas Aquinas, as argued by George Weigel in *The Cube and the Cathedral*, are central in providing 'a bridge in European culture between the classical world and the medieval world (one that) yielded a rich, complex and deeply humanistic vision of the human person, human goods, human society and human destiny'.

And central to Aquinas' philosophy, as stated by Pope John Paul in 'Fides et Ratio', is 'the courage of the truth, a freedom of spirit in confronting new problems, the intellectual honesty of those who allow Christianity to be contaminated neither by secular philosophy nor by a prejudiced rejection of it'.

Aryan Hirsi Ali, the Somalian activist who writes extensively on the dangers of fundamentalist forms of Islam, when interviewed on the ABC earlier this year argues that to fight terrorism the West must 'inculcate into the minds and hearts of young people an ideology or ideas of life, love, peace and tolerance'.

While a military response and anti-terrorism strategies like increased surveillance are vital, equally as important is the need to defend the values Hirsi Ali refers to; values that are essential characteristics of Western, liberal democracies like Australia.

Christianity crucified while Islam is idolised

The Daily Telegraph
17 December 2015

In his speech linking fundamentalist Islam with terrorism Tony Abbott argued that we in the West, and especially Australia, need 'a concerted hearts and minds campaign' against Islamic terrorism.

And one of the key areas linked to such a campaign is how religion is being taught in the school curriculum.

In Britain, Prime Minister David Cameron argues Britain is a Christian nation and all schools must teach religion and British values. In response to the terrorist incidents in Sydney the NSW government earlier this year investigated prayer groups.

In order to promote tolerance the Victorian government is introducing ethical capability into the curriculum where students will be 'introduced to different religions and world views and a range of relevant philosophers and/or schools of thought'.

Last year's review of the Australian National Curriculum also recommended there be a greater emphasis on 'morals, values and spirituality' and 'the contribution of Western civilisation (and) our Judeo-Christian heritage'.

While the consensus is that students need to learn more about religion, based on events both here and in the UK, there are a number of potential dangers.

One danger is a relativistic position is adopted where all religions are considered of equal value and significance.

Not true. While Abrahamic religions (Judaism, Islam and Christianity) share common origins, they are fundamentally different.

The Koran is not the Bible and the New Testament is not the Torah. Australia, while increasingly multicultural, is essentially a Western, liberal democratic nation that owes more to Judeo-Christianity than to Islam, Hinduism or Buddhism.

At the time of Federation more than 90 per cent of those surveyed described themselves as Christian and, as argued by Perth academic Augusto Zimmerman, 'Judeo-Christian values were so embedded in Australia so as to necessitate the recognition of God in the nation's founding document … it is evident the foundations of the Australian nation, and its laws, have discernible Christian-philosophical roots'.

Concepts such as sanctity of life, individual conscience and free will, a commitment to the common good and the importance of forgiveness and the possibility of redemption are Christian in origin.

As argued by Somali-born Ayaan Hirsi Ali, it is also the case, unlike Christianity where the Bible states 'render to Caesar the things that are Caesar's', there is no separation between church and state in the Koran.

The second danger is that teaching about religion in schools is one-sided. Textbooks such as Jacaranda's *SOSE Alive 2*, Oxford University Press's *Big Ideas Australian Curriculum History 8* emphasise the dark side of Christianity when referring to the Inquisition, burning witches and relying on fear to win converts.

Learning From One Another: Bringing Muslim Perspectives into Australian Schools published by Melbourne University, on the other hand, presents a sanitised version of Islam.

Students are told 'jihad' refers to a 'spiritual struggle' and, while it may involve armed fighting, it is generally only 'in self-defence'.

When detailing the spread of Islam across Europe the textbook also states nonbelievers 'were allowed to live peacefully and practise their faith as long as they abided by the law of the land'. Ignored is Islam's involvement in slavery and the fact those who refused to convert were put to death or lost their freedom, the right to own property and to practise their religion.

The Australian national curriculum History and Civics and Citizenship documents are also biased in that, while students must learn about Indigenous spirituality, Christianity is airbrushed from the nation's history.

In the Civics curriculum there is no mention of the Christian charities, philanthropic bodies and organisations that represent a vital part of Australia's education, health, welfare and social service sectors.

As proven by the forced closure of a number of Christian schools in Britain, as a result of supposedly failing to abide by the government's orders about teaching religious beliefs and British values, it is also true teaching religion can have unintended consequences. One school was criticised for being Islamophobic and another for failing to implement the government's cultural-Left sexuality and gender agenda.

To raise the above caveats does not mean religion should not be in the school curriculum; rather it has to be taught in an objective, balanced and impartial manner.

As noted by T. S. Eliot, religion is an essential element of any culture and this is especially true with Western civilisation as: 'It is in Christianity that our arts have developed; it is in Christianity that the laws of Europe have, until recently, been rooted. It is against a background of Christianity that all our thought has significance'.

We must never forget the good work of Christianity

The Herald Sun
8 March 2016

There's no doubt it's a hard time being a Christian, especially if you are
a Catholic. As Cardinal Pell admitted during his interview with Andrew
Bolt, many in the Church failed to confront the evil of child abuse
and what happened destroyed the lives of hundreds of innocent and
vulnerable children.

Add the fact that secular critics like Richard Dawkins and Christopher
Hitchens argue believing in God is infantile and faith equals superstition
and it's understandable why some, like Elise Elliot, turn their back on the
Church (*Herald Sun*, 24 February).

I was also raised as a Catholic but, unlike Elliot, I have not forsaken the
Church and what Christianity and the Bible offer.

Growing up in working class Broadmeadows during the '60s wasn't
easy and having an alcoholic, violent father didn't make things any better.
But mother's faith, Mass on Sunday and prayer provided solace and the
belief there is good in the world.

Each night, before sleep, I would recite 'Now I lay me down to sleep,
I pray the Lord my soul to keep and if I die before I wake I pray to God
my soul to take' and prayed that life would not always be so painful and
difficult.

The Bible taught me there is evil in human nature and that we are
all open to temptation and sin but at the same time the parables taught

me about goodness, sacrificing oneself for others, redemption and the importance of having courage and being resilient.

Parables like the 'Good Samaritan' and the 'Prodigal Son' describe in a succinct and direct way important moral lessons like always helping others. Expressions like 'turn the other cheek' and 'let him whom is without sin cast the first stone' helped me understand human nature and the importance of forgiveness.

Communion and confirmation at St Dominic's in Camp Road gave me a sense of belonging to something more significant and lasting by opening a transcendent world of ritual, mystery and faith.

And for those who believe that science dispels mystery and faith Albert Einstein writes 'The fairest thing we can experience is the mysterious. It is the fundamental emotion that stands at the cradle of true art and true science... It was the experience of mystery — even with mixed with fear — that engendered religion... in this sense, and in this alone, I am a deeply religious man'.

There's no doubt that to be human is to suffer good and evil, joy and pain and love and loss. And for a parent there is no greater tragedy than losing a son or daughter. Such was the case when our son, James, was killed in a hit and run while walking home from a mate's party.

And again, it is religion that I turned to. Faith provides the belief that there is a world beyond this one and offers comfort and the hope that all is not lost.

The Christian mystic, Julian of Norwich, also points to an essential truth when she writes 'But we cannot escape the suffering and the sorrow: there are dark sides to life. Realism forces us to face the fact. And the same realism enables us to trust the light and life and love in which we are enfolded'.

While nothing will ever erase the suffering and pain of losing a son, religion and the words of Christian mystics like Julian of Norwich provide solace and a sense that we are all a part of something larger and beneficial.

No one can deny the fact that there are evil priests who victimised and destroyed the lives of innocent children and young men and women. At the same time it is vital to acknowledge the profound and ongoing debt owed to Christianity and the Church.

Catholic schools across Australia enrol 20% of students, charitable organisations like the Salvation Army and World Vision help millions of the poor and disadvantaged both here and overseas.

Whether health, medicine, social welfare or helping those who are victims of domestic violence or drug abuse it is Christian groups and bodies like Compassion Australia and the St Vincent de Paul Society that underpin Australia's social services and welfare sector and without which governments would be unable to cope.

The English poet and mystic William Blake, while no defender of organised religion, argues 'He who sees the Infinite in all things sees God. He who sees the Ratio only sees himself only'.

Elliot concludes her piece by writing 'And I won't open the heavy doors of church ever again'. For me that is not an option. It is by opening the doors that we enter a rich, spiritual world that transcends the present and offers balm to a weary soul.

Let's celebrate the role of Christianity in our culture

The Herald Sun
12 April 2017

Proven by the celebration of Easter, while we are a secular society we are also a culture deeply influenced by Christianity and the Bible.

T. S. Eliot, the English poet whose work inspired the musical Cats, argues Christianity underpins much of Western civilisation, including our legal and political systems, the concept of public and private morality and our literature and the arts.

When detailing what makes Western culture unique, Eliot argues: 'It is against a background of Christianity that all our thought has significance', and goes as far as arguing, 'if Christianity goes, the whole of our culture goes'.

Whereas Muslim cultures worship the Koran, Hindus the Vedas, Buddhists the Sutras and Jews the Torah, the foundation text for Western culture is the story of Christ detailed in the Bible.

The English language, especially our literature, owes much to the Bible, especially the New Testament. Expressions like 'turn the other cheek', 'be a good Samaritan', 'let he who is without sin cast the first stone', 'the blind leading the blind' and 'pride comes before the fall' are all derived from the Bible. Literary texts like *The Canterbury Tales*, *Pilgrims Progress*, Dante's *Divine Comedy* and more modern examples like the Narnia books by C. S. Lewis, Patrick White's *Voss* and Tim Winton's *Cloudstreet* cannot be fully appreciated without knowledge of Christian beliefs and values.

Western art, proven by Michelangelo's *Pieta* and the *Sistine Chapel* and Leonardo da Vinci's *The Last Supper* and *The Annunciation*, draws heavily on Biblical references. Famous and enduring composers like Handel, Bach, Beethoven and Faure, in the same way, were inspired by Christian teachings.

Australia's political and legal systems, like those in the UK and America, also draw heavily on Christian morality and the Ten Commandments.

The *American Declaration of Independence* describes the right to 'Life, Liberty and the pursuit of Happiness' as God-given and it's no accident that banknotes are printed with the phrase 'In God We Trust'.

As argued by the Perth-based legal academic, Augusto Zimmerman, the moment Governor Phillip landed at Sydney Cove and planted the British flag, we inherited a legal and political system heavily influenced by Christianity and the Bible.

Zimmerman writes: 'It is evident that the foundations of the Australian nation, and its laws, have discernible Christian-philosophical roots' and this explains why the Preamble to the Australian Constitution includes the words 'humbly relying on the blessing of Almighty God'.

The Biblical statement 'There is neither Jew nor Greek, there is neither bond nor free, there is neither male nor female: for ye are all one in Christ Jesus' forms the basis for Western legal and political concepts like the inherent dignity of each person and the right to freedom and liberty.

In a world where millions are denied the freedoms we take for granted, the fact that Australia is a Western liberal democracy heavily influenced by Christianity explains why so many migrants want to immigrate here and lead a free life.

The belief that we are made in God's image explains the value our culture places on the sanctity of life and the commandment to 'Love thy neighbour as thyself' is the reason so many charitable and philanthropic organisations are Christian. According to some estimates nearly 50 per cent of Australia's health, education, social welfare and charitable organisations are either Christian or Christian in origin. With schools, for example, more than 20 per cent of Australian students are taught in Catholic schools.

Julia Gillard, when prime minister, and even though an atheist, stressed the value of the Bible when she argued it 'formed such an important part of our culture' and that 'it is impossible to understand Western literature without that key of understanding the Bible stories and how Western literature builds on them'.

With home invasions, domestic violence, car thefts, street violence and robberies on the increase it's clear that many in society lack a moral compass and while the Bible is not the sole arbiter of what constitutes right and wrong, it represents an essential place to start.

Given the threat of Islamic terrorism and the way extremists use the Koran to justify their jihad against the West, it is even more vital that we acknowledge how the Bible underpins our way of life.

This year marks the 200th anniversary of the Bible Society of Australia and there is no doubt the Bible has had, and continues to have, a significant impact on our way of life.

Faith still a key to complete life

The Sunday Herald Sun
24 December 2017

Best illustrated by the celebration of Christmas and the birth of Jesus, it's easy to imagine it's a good time to be religious and to declare one's faith. Not so. Given the increasing secularisation of society where materialism and narcissism reign and where critics claim religion has no place in public debates like same-sex marriage and euthanasia, it's clear that Christianity is under attack.

It's not unusual for schools to ban Christian hymns and nativity scenes on the basis that we are multicultural and for Christmas cards to wish 'a Merry Christmas' without any mention or reference to the birth of Christ.

And it's not just that society is changing as a result of fewer Christians attending church and about 30 per cent of Australians identifying as non-religious. Given the unforgivable child abuse revealed by the royal commission, an Ipsos survey found 63 per cent of Australians believe 'religion does more harm than good'.

But in turning our backs on religion and criticising Judeo-Christianity in particular, the question has to be asked: what have we lost and if religion disappears, what will take its place?

Some now argue the Western world has entered a post-Christian age where secular values and beliefs dominate. Religion is condemned as obsolete. Critics, such as Liberal MP Christopher Pyne, also mistakenly argue there is no place for Christianity in society as our institutions are based on the separation between church and state. Unlike theocracies like Islamic Iran and Afghanistan where religious Imams rule, Western democracies do not allow priests to govern.

Ignored is that it's impossible to understand Australian society without some knowledge of how Christianity underpins our way of life. While we are a secular society, religion is pervasive.

Religious events like Christmas and Easter are obvious examples.

As argued by the Perth-based academic Augusto Zimmerman, our political and legal systems and institutions draw heavily on Christianity, especially the New Testament. The biblical statement, 'There is neither Jew nor Greek, there is neither bond nor free, there is neither male nor female: for ye are all one in Christ Jesus', is based on the belief in the inherent dignity of each person and the God given right to liberty and freedom.

Even those not committed to any religious faith, in arguing that tolerance, respect for others and equality before the law are paramount, whether they acknowledge it or not, are drawing on Christian beliefs and virtues.

Christianity, especially in times of sorrow, uncertainty and loss, provides a sense that even though this world is not perfect it is possible to find solace and what the poet T. S. Eliot calls 'the peace which passes all understanding'.

Such is the need for a more transcendent and spiritual sense of life that the 20th century's most famous scientist Albert Einstein argued that experiencing what he describes as 'mysterious' is central to human nature. Einstein argued that religion is important and that 'whoever does not know it and can no longer wonder, no longer marvel, is as good as dead, and his eyes are dimmed'.

Atheist Douglas Murray argues that religion should not be ignored — he says he is a cultural Christian on the basis that to appreciate Western culture is to recognise the importance of Christianity.

Those who have lost loved ones, especially in tragic and unexpected circumstances, know the need to seek comfort and reassurance in something higher and more lasting than this transitory existence.

Great art and music like da Vinci's *The Last Supper*, Handel's *Messiah* and Michelangelo's *The Sistine Chapel* draw heavily on Christianity and in achieving the sublime, draw closer to God.

And, as research is beginning to prove, this sense of spirituality and understanding cannot be found in today's digital world where so many are surrounded by ego-driven social networking sites and applications that breed isolation and lack of real engagement.

Each week research shows high rates of suicide, self-harm and depression. Ever younger children complain of sexting, cyber bullying and feeling uncertain and anxious.

Basic norms of civil behaviour like respecting others, being polite and living according to the biblical admonition 'do unto others as you would have them do unto you' appear all but forgotten.

Worst still, as a result of cultural amnesia we run the risk of no longer knowing who we are and what is most worth conserving.

Take it as gospel, the good book is key to learning

The Australian
27 February 2018

Tony Abbott and Julia Gillard don't have a lot in common, apart from leading the nation, but when it comes to including the Bible in the school curriculum both are singing from the same hymn book.

As prime minister, Gillard argued in 2011 that the Bible was 'an important part of our culture' and that 'it's impossible to understand Western literature without having that key of understanding the Bible stories'.

Abbott, a year earlier when leader of the opposition, argued in a similar fashion when he said 'it is impossible to imagine our society without the influence of Christendom' and 'it is important for people to leave school with some understanding of the Bible'.

While secular critics argue there is no place for Christianity and the Bible in the school curriculum the arguments in favour are overwhelming. As stated by Professor Higgins when admonishing Eliza, 'your native language is the language of Shakespeare and Milton and the Bible'.

The *King James Bible* is considered by many as an example of the English language at its most evocative and powerful, and explains why Michael Gove, as British education secretary, sent a copy to every school in the country.

Classical tales such as Bunyan's *The Pilgrim's Progress*, Chaucer's *Canterbury Tales*, and more recent literature including Dostoyevsky's *The*

Brothers Karamazov, T. S. Eliot's *The Journey of the Magi* and Tim Winton's *Cloudstreet* all require a knowledge and understanding of the Bible.

And it goes without saying that much of Western culture's music, art and architecture reference Christianity and cannot be fully appreciated without some familiarity with the Old and New Testaments and the story of Christ.

Sayings and proverbs such as 'turn the other cheek', 'be a good Samaritan', 'let him who is without sin cast the first stone' and 'the blind leading the blind' are derived from the Bible.

As important in a time of rampant materialism, anxiety and angst caused by social media and the new technologies, stories from the Bible also teach students the importance of a more transcendent and spiritual sense of life.

In the same way the national curriculum stipulates students should learn about Indigenous religion and spirituality, as our way of life is steeped in Western culture and underpinned by Judeo-Christianity, it's only reasonable and fair that the Bible is also in the curriculum.

Virtues versus vague values

Spectator Australia
15 December 2018

Which is preferable: values or virtues? The question might appear overly academic and of little relevance but how it is answered has had, and continues to have, a profound impact on Australia's education system and our way of life.

One approach is best illustrated by a flyer titled *Values for Australian Schooling* that was circulated to all schools when John Howard was Prime Minister. The impetus for the flyer was the Prime Minister's belief that more needed to be done to provide students with a more explicit moral and ethical framework when deciding right from wrong and what constitutes good and bad behaviour.

The values promoted were: care and compassion, doing your best, fair go, freedom, honesty and trustworthiness, integrity, respect, responsibility, understanding, tolerance and inclusion. The impetus to teach values is further evidenced by the publication in 2005 of the 'National Framework for Values Education in Australian Schools' and, more recently, the way values education is incorporated into the national curriculum.

Three of the general capabilities informing all subjects from the preparatory year to year 10 are personal and social capability, ethical understanding and intercultural understanding. All involve identifying and teaching politically correct values such as respecting diversity and difference, tolerating other cultures, caring for the environment and being good global citizens.

Like motherhood, the first thing to note about the aforementioned values is that they are uncontroversial and, on first reading, appear worthwhile and beneficial. Freedom, honesty, respecting others and being a responsible citizen are all commendable. While such values can be criticised for being self-evident and bland there is little to disagree with.

On a closer examination there is cause for concern. Respecting others, being inclusive and acknowledging diversity and difference should never mean tolerating the intolerable. Some cultural practices and some forms of behaviour are morally offensive and unacceptable.

Those who migrate to Australia, for example, should accept and abide by our laws and way of life and not import unacceptable customs such as female circumcision and child brides. Cultural relativism leads to societal fragmentation and disunity and what Geoffrey Blainey once called the danger of becoming a nation of tribes.

A further criticism, notwithstanding the widespread use of values as denoting what constitutes an acceptable moral and ethical framework, is that its use cannot disguise the fact that the attributes listed are vague and insubstantial.

They lack an explicit, clear and compelling moral underpinning. Iain T. Benson from Australia's Notre Dame University argues using the term values is misleading and dangerous as it is a 'vague term that introduces subjective confusion into moral claims'. For all the talk about values, whether in education, politics or the world of business, Benson argues that it is impossible to advocate or defend values without evaluating the underlying ethical and moral framework.

Benson goes on to argue 'the language of values obscures reality' and its widespread use is being employed 'to drive religion and its moral language to the margins of culture'. In a secular, supposedly post-Christian age where cultural-left theory prevails employing the language of values undermines Christianity in an attempt to banish it from the public square.

In opposition to values Benson mounts a case for what he terms virtues. He argues 'values and virtues are utterly different creatures' on the basis that 'Virtues are thick and entailed and have a content and long traditions spanning countries, philosophies and religions: values are thin, unentailed and, well, whatever you want them to be'.

Drawing on the Christian faith Benson cites the cardinal virtues as an explicit, enduring and compelling description of a moral and ethical framework that is closely associated with the history and evolution of Western civilisation and Australia's cultural heritage.

The virtues listed include 'justice, wisdom, moderation and courage'. Added to this list are what Benson describes as the theological virtues of 'faith, hope and love'. Virtues, by their very nature, stipulate a strong and consistent moral code not based on personal feelings or capable of changing from day to day depending on the situation.

Significant, given the politically correct national curriculum we now have where relativism and subjectivity prevail, is that Benson refers to John Dewey the father of progressive, new-age education when explaining the prevalence of a values approach.

Dewey, who was a strong secular advocate, argues there is no place for Christianity in what he describes as 'the realization of the democratic ideal'. His views on education underpin much of the current progressive approach; one that argues the curriculum must be contemporary, immediately relevant and based on the world of the child.

In *Thinking Christian Ethos* published by the Catholic Trust Society in London a strong case is also put for ensuring that virtues as opposed to values are centre stage and that they underpin what is taught and how schools are managed and organised.

The authors, drawing on the writings of Plato, Aristotle and Thomas Aquinas, describe what they term as a moral virtue 'as a settled disposition to react in the right way and do the right thing, to do what promotes the true flourishing of human persons'. Such virtues are listed as 'courage, temperateness, justice and good sense'.

Education, by its very nature is inherently moral and as argued by *Thinking Christian Ethos* it should involve 'the cultivation of the moral and intellectual virtues, for the good of the person and for the common good of society'.

Given the prevalence of values in education, made worse by the impact of cultural-left theory involving a heady blend of Neo-Marxism, feminism, postmodernism, deconstructionism and gender and post-colonial theories, it's understandable why what is taught is so superficial and lacking in moral substance and integrity.

The curriculum no longer inculcates justice, wisdom, moderation and courage. Even worse because education no longer deals with virtues increasing numbers of students lack a moral compass and leave school with an ego centred, narcissistic sense of self and their place in the wider world.

Here's why we celebrate

The Daily Telegraph
19 December 2018

Walk into department store, shopping mall or down most suburban streets and it's obvious what time of year it is. Christmas decorations, jingles like *Rudolf the Red Nosed Reindeer* and portrayals of Father Christmas abound.

But Christmas is not just about Santa Claus. Even though most of the displays and decorations ignore the Three Wise Men and the nativity scene the reality is that Christmas celebrates the birth of Christ. An event signally the arrival of Christianity and a moral and spiritual framework that underpins and nurtures our institutions and way of life.

All cultures have a religion. In the Middle East it's Islam, in China Confucianism, and India Buddhism. In Western, liberal democracies like Australia it is Christianity and the New Testament.

The fact that we are a Christian nation instead of being ignored should be cause for celebration. The freedoms and liberties we all take for granted derive largely from the Christian belief that we are all made in God's image.

The expression from the Bible 'There is neither Jew nor Gentile, neither slave nor free, nor is there male and female, for you are all one in Christ Jesus' encapsulates the Christian belief in the inherent dignity of the person.

While Christianity, like other religions, has been guilty of great sins it also has the saving grace of being able to overcome past injustices and wrongs. Those responsible for abolishing slavery in England all those years ago were Christians and their weapon was the Bible.

It's no surprise that the *American Declaration of Independence* states each person's right to be treated equally and to enjoy 'life, liberty and the pursuit of happiness' are 'endowed by their creator'. The impact of Christianity is also proven by the fact that our parliaments begin with the Lord's Prayer.

As argued by Perth-based academic Augusto Zimmermann, Christianity also underpins and informs our legal system. The right to be judged according to the law and not to be held or imprisoned without cause can be traced back to 'Magna Carta' and the belief that the King was not above God.

Unlike Islam that is a theocracy where there is no division between church and state it is also true that Christianity differentiates between the Church and the secular state. As Christ spoke 'Render unto Caesar the things that are Caesar's, and unto God the things that are God's'.

The division between Church and state ensures that neither religion nor government act alone in seeking to control the citizen, both have an essential and important role to play. Unlike many Islamic states where the government is either controlled or made up of religious leaders.

The birth and story of Christ also is important as it teaches us that there is more to this life than material satisfaction and being ego centred. While the emphasis of Christmas is very much on buying and receiving presents it is vital to realise that there is a greater and more lasting gift on hand.

Christianity is a religion that offers a spiritual and transcendent sense of life. This material world is transitory and one dimensional. Christmas presents soon lose their appeal and no amount of possessions can guard against the challenges and tragedies experienced on life's journey.

To go through life without being touched by tragedy caused by the death of a loved one or suffering a life-threatening illness or personal loss is so rare it's like winning the lottery. Christianity offers solace and comfort as it teaches that suffering and pain are an inescapable part of life. At the same time faith teaches there is a more transcendent world and all is not lost.

The English Christian mystic Julian of Norwich suggests this when she writes as a result of her love and commitment to Christ 'All shall be well, and all shall be well and all manner of things shall be well'.

That Christianity is such a source of inspiration and hope is proven by the great works of art, music and architecture. Anyone who has stood in front of Michelangelo's *Pieta* or admired his painting of the Sistine Chapel will understand there is a higher inspiration.

Bach's *Mass in B Minor* and Handel's *Messiah* are also imbued with a deep and lasting sense of religion and of the spiritual and sublime. It's no accident that communist and fascist states where Christianity was banned never achieved comparable works of music and art.

Christmas is a time for reunions, giving a receiving gifts and enjoying too much food and wine. At the time we should also remember the birth of Christ and why Christianity is vital to our way of life.

In our secular society, virtues must trump vapid, subjective values

The Australian
1 January 2019

Virtues or values? In what has become a more secular society devoid of any reference to religion or what constitutes a transcendent and spiritual sense of morality and what constitutes the good life and the common good, values are centre stage.

In schools and universities, in businesses across Australia, and among politicians and in public debate, values such as compassion, a fair go, respecting diversity and difference and being honest and trustworthy are continually referred to as beneficial and worthy of emulation.

While initially attractive and worthwhile, such statements, on closer examination, prove to be vapid and superficial.

Respecting diversity and difference, the new code for multiculturalism, should never mean tolerating the intolerable.

Some cultural practices are inimical to our way of life and should not be allowed. It's also true that values are often subjective and relative, as they lack a defining and consistent ethical and moral framework.

Iain T. Benson from Australia's Notre Dame University best sums up the flawed nature of values when he writes 'the language of values obscures reality' as values 'is a vague term that introduces subjective confusion into moral claims'.

What constitutes a fair go can vary depending on one's political beliefs. The socialist mantra 'from each according to his ability, to each according to his needs' justifies state intervention on the basis that private property is theft and that the collective must be in control.

Such a definition is the opposite of former British Prime Minister Margaret Thatcher's statement: 'And, you know, there's no such thing as society. There are individual men and women and there are families. And no government can do anything except through people, and people must look after themselves first. It is our duty to look after ourselves and then, also, to look after our neighbours.'

Whereas values are difficult to define as they vary and lack a rigorous and credible moral framework, virtues have the benefit of being consistent and grounded in a strong sense of morality and, but not exclusively, religious teachings.

As David Albert Jones and Stephen Barrie write in *Thinking Christian Ethos*, the concept of virtues defining right and wrong and what constitutes the good life and how best to contribute to the common good can be traced back to Plato and Aristotle.

Aristotle argued that to live well and flourish requires living virtuously by adopting character traits grounded in virtues such as courage, magnanimity, liberality, truthfulness and justice. Such virtues do not arise intuitively or by accident, and require an education that exemplifies virtues and teaches what constitutes virtuous conduct.

The theologian St Thomas Aquinas, while drawing on the philosophy of the early Greeks, provides a uniquely Christian view of virtues based on the teachings of Christ as revealed in the New Testament. Described as the cardinal virtues, these include prudence, temperance, courage and justice.

It goes without saying that the virtues Aquinas espoused are deeply religious in nature and rely on a spiritual and transcendent view of life and the power and authenticity of the word of God as revealed in admonitions such as: 'Thou shalt love thy neighbour as thyself.'

In addition to Christianity, the concept of virtues has also had a profound impact on what constitutes a liberal view of education. Matthew Arnold in *Culture and Anarchy* says education is about character and teaching 'the best that has been thought and said' and inculcating a commitment to 'sweetness and light'.

Cardinal John Henry Newman, in *The Idea of a University*, defines and illustrates virtues when he writes the true purpose of education is to promote 'freedom, equitableness, calmness, moderation, and wisdom; or what in a previous discourse I have ventured to call a philosophical habit'.

As to whether virtues or values are preferable and whether one provides a more beneficial, positive and rewarding moral framework is not just an academic exercise. The reality is that central to any culture is the moral and ethical belief system that determines its way of life and how individuals live and interact with others.

And judged by what is happening in Australia, it's clear that the prevalence of values is far from beneficial and worthwhile. Our political system is driven by personal ambition, hubris and animosity rather than a commitment to the common good and what constitutes right and wrong behaviour.

The corrupt, dishonest and self-serving actions of the banks and other financial corporations revealed by last year's royal commission also highlight what happens when virtues such as truthfulness and justice no longer apply.

As illustrated by cultural-Left academics at the Australian National University and the University of Sydney rejecting the proposal to establish a Western civilisation centre funded by the bequest left by Paul Ramsay, it's also clear that Newman's definition no longer applies.

Instead of truth and wisdom, universities with rare exceptions are riven with destructive and nihilistic ideologies represented by postmodernism, deconstructionism, neo-Marxist and postcolonial, feminist and gender and sexuality theories.

The fact that values fail to provide a sustaining and enriching sense of morality and how to deal with the existential challenges we all face is highlighted by the ever-increasing rates of self-harm, anxiety, suicide and drug use across society — especially among the young.

Why not 'welcome to Christianity'?

Spectator Australia
13 July 2019

Imagine the outcry by the inner-city limousine left and the free-trade, almond latte drinkers if the Victorian Labor government decided to ban the welcome to country greeting at the start of each parliamentary sitting.

Even the suggestion that politicians no longer acknowledge Victoria's first inhabitants would cause a tidal wave of complaint reinforced by the left-leaning commentariat at the ABC and *The Age*. Acknowledging Aboriginal history, culture and spirituality for many is the new religion.

But when it comes to the Andrews Government's intention to abolish the century old practice of reciting the Lord's Prayer all are silent. Such is the dominance of soulless, secular ideology that Christianity is seen as obsolete and irrelevant.

Ignored is that Christianity is central to Australia's history and evolution as a nation. Concepts like the inherent dignity of each person, a commitment to the common good and seeking good instead of evil are all derived from the New Testament.

As argued by Larry Siedentop in *The Origins of Western Liberalism* Christ's teachings revolutionised Western societies by introducing the belief that what the *American Declaration of Independence* describes as the right to 'life, liberty and the pursuit of happiness' is God given.

All are equal before the eyes of God and while Christianity has not always lived up to the ideal the duty of each person is to respect others and to try and live a life characterised by humility, truthfulness and compassion.

The admonition from the Bible 'There is neither Jew nor Gentile, neither slave nor free, nor is there male and female, for you are all one in Christ Jesus' best illustrates the Christian commitment to treating all with kindness, justice and respect.

Christianity is especially central to the political and legal institutions we have inherited from England. Our Westminster Parliamentary system where the monarch no longer rules, each citizen has the right to vote and to live a life free of unjustified government intervention is underpinned by Christianity.

Informing 'Magna Carta' is the Christian belief that as the monarch is answerable to the laws of God he or she must abide by what is right and just. When summarising the impact of the New Testament on the beginnings of the Westminster system the legal academic John C.H. Wu writes: 'If the king does justice he is a minister of God; if he does injustice, he becomes an agent of the devil. He is above his people, but he is under God and under the Law, for it is the Law that makes him King'.

Our legal system where all have the right to a fair trial and are innocent until proven guilty also draws heavily on the New Testament. As argued by the Perth based legal academic Augusto Zimmermann, the author of *Christian Foundations of the Common Law*.

'When considered alongside the development of colonial laws, the adoption of the English common-law tradition and American system of federation, it is evident that the foundations of the Australian nation, and its laws, have discernible Christian-philosophical roots'.

No amount of debate about the rights and wrongs of Australia Day celebrating the arrival of the First Fleet will ever change the fact that British common law and the Bible arrived at the same time as the first convicts, thus, guaranteeing legal protection for all.

Even though Australia is increasingly multi-cultural and multi-faith the reality is that we are a Western liberal democracy where Christianity is the dominant religion and our way of life is deeply imbued with Christian beliefs and morality.

And it's not just our political and legal institutions. Christian schools, hospitals, aged care facilities and social welfare and community organisations are either Christian inspired or Christian managed.

Research puts the figure at approximately 50 per cent and without Christianity's ongoing contribution there is no doubt that state, territory and commonwealth governments would be unable to cope and communities would suffer and our way of life deteriorate.

Catholic and other Christian schools, for example, enrol approximately 34% of students across Australia thus saving state and commonwealth governments billions each and every year as students in such schools are not fully funded by the state.

Much of our music, literature and art is also heavily influence by Christianity and can only be fully understood and appreciated in the context of the story of Christ. Examples include Handel's *Messiah*, C. S. Lewis' Narnia trilogy, the novels of Tim Winton and Michelangelo's *Sistine Chapel*.

As argued by the English poet T S Eliot 'It is in Christianity that our arts have developed; it is in Christianity that the laws of Europe have – until recently – been rooted. It is against a background of Christianity that all our thought has significance'.

Eliot also makes the point that a culture without religion is one bereft of any sense of the spiritual and the transcendent and one where materialism and nihilism will reign supreme.

It is also important to recognise that the move to scrap the Lord's Prayer is part of a larger cultural-left, secular attack on Christianity by various governments. Last year the Victorian government removed religious education from the formal school curriculum while forcing schools to implement radical gender and sexuality programs.

The Australian Capital Territory some years ago removed the Lord's Prayer from its parliament and the policy of the Greens Party is also to banish such a ritual at the commonwealth level.

The policies of the Australian Labor Party and the Greens Party involve restricting religious freedom by denying the right currently exercised by faith-based schools to decide what they teach and how their schools are managed and organised.

If Bill Shorten becomes Australia's next prime minister, as the polls suggest, then expect and even more secular, Marxist inspired attack on religious freedom and the right each citizen has to express and live by their beliefs.

There are even those secular critics who argue there is no place for religion in public debate or public policy; especially with issues like same-sex marriage, abortion and so-called mercy killing.

It's ironic that at the same time the cultural-left celebrates and lauds Aboriginal culture, history and spirituality it is doing all in its power to destroy the Christian faith and to deny the existence of what is an essential and critical part of Australia's mainstream culture.

Christianity is at the heart of the West

The Herald Sun
9 September 2019

The Scott Morrison government has just released its draft freedom of religion bill and already debates have begun about whether it goes far enough to protect religious freedom. On one hand religious organisations like the Catholic Church argue the draft bill is flawed as it does not recognise religious freedom as a positive right.

On the other hand others argue religious freedom is only one freedom among many that must be restricted. Religious schools, for example, must not discriminate when it comes to employing staff and employees like Israel Folau contracted to Rugby Australia cannot make public religious beliefs that harm their employer's business.

One of the most common arguments curtailing religious freedom is that Australia is a secular society. Peter Van Onselen, for example, argues it is wrong to treat religious faith as a positive right because we are 'living in a secular society' (*Weekend Australian*, 31 August).

While many secular critics yearn for a post-Christian age where the word of God no longer exists and Christians are banished to eke out their existence on the fringes of society the reality is that to deny the relevance of Christianity is to rewrite history and to destroy the fabric of Western civilisation.

As argued by T. S. Eliot in *Notes Towards a Definition of Culture* religion is an essential and inherent part of any culture, especially in relation to

Western civilisations like Australia where Eliot argues 'If Christianity goes, the whole of our culture goes'.

Douglas Murray in *The Strange Death of Europe* makes a similar point when arguing that Europe's 'self-supporting structure of rights, laws and institutions' could not exist without Christianity as 'the source that had arguably given them life'.

Anyone with a knowledge of English language and literature will understand Christianity and the Bible have had, and continue to have, a profound influence. Everyday expressions like 'turn the other cheek', 'the prodigal son', 'can a leopard change its spots' and 'forbidden fruit' are biblical in origin.

Literary works central to the Western canon including Bunyan's *The Pilgrims Progress*, Dante's *Divine Comedy*, Milton's *Paradise Lost*, Shakespeare's tragedies and more recently the works of Dostoevsky, T.S. Eliot, Patrick White and Tim Winton are all steeped in Christianity.

Great literature deals with enduring moral and spiritual dilemmas involving sin, temptation, guilt, redemption and atonement that can only be fully understood in the context of the New Testament and the life and words of Jesus the Christ.

The political and legal systems we have inherited from England can also only be understood in terms of Christian beliefs and faith. Such systems draw largely on a Westminster parliamentary system and English common law that can be traced back to 'Magna Carta', the Glorious revolution and the various reform and emancipation acts.

Those responsible for the steady increase in liberty and freedom were often deeply religious and as written by Winston Churchill in his *A History of the English Speaking Peoples* when detailing the significance of 'Magna Carta', Christianity played a major role as 'the King should not be below man, but below God and the law'.

The importance of Christianity explains why parliaments begin with the Lord's Prayer and why the Preamble to the Australian constitution includes the phrase 'Humbly relying on the blessing of Almighty God'.

The *American Declaration of Independence* argues the right to 'Life, Liberty and the pursuit of Happiness' are inherent rights 'endowed by their creator'. Larry Siedentop in *Inventing the Individual: The Origins of Western Liberalism* provides a compelling and persuasive account of how Christianity underpins the right to equality, justice and freedom.

The New Testament introduced into Western thought the conviction that as all individuals are made in God's image they have inherent rights that must be protected. Concepts like free will, moral agency, freedom of conscience and justice for all are largely derived from Christian beliefs and teachings.

As argued by the Italian philosopher Augusto Del Noce , what many secular critics conveniently ignore is that taken to its logical conclusion the denial of 'traditional morality and religion' where there is no longer any transcendent truth or higher purpose can lead to totalitarian dictatorships.

The belief that nothing exists above man's law and utopia can be created on this earth has led to the starvation, torture, subjugation and death of countless millions. Beginning with the French Revolution and continuing with Nazi Germany, Stalin's Russia, Mao's China and Pol Pot's killing fields history proves the danger of denying Christianity its rightful place.

Saint embraced an education that seeks wisdom and truth

The Catholic Weekly
11 October 2019

The English paster, educator, theologian and historian John Henry Newman is to be declared a saint by Pope Francis at the Vatican Sunday October the 13th. Initially ordained as a Church of England priest Newman founded the Oxford movement before converting to Catholicism in 1845.

While renowned as an orator, philosopher and theologian one of his most lasting legacies is a series of lectures titled the *Idea of a University*. Unlike the majority of today's universities consumed by corporate managerialism, cultural-left political correctness and tenured radicals Newman embraces what he describes as a liberal education.

Newman defines this as a 'process of training, by which the intellect, instead of being formed or sacrificed to some particular or accidental purpose, some specific trade or profession, or study of science, is disciplined for its own sake, for the perception of its own proper object, and for its own highest culture'.

Newman's starting point is that knowledge does not arise intuitively or by accident and that a university education should be directed at the 'cultivation of the intellect'.

Unlike Marxist inspired critical theory, postmodernism and deconstructionism Newman's ideal is one that seeks wisdom and truth.

An education 'pursued for its own sake' and one where 'Truth of whatever kind is the proper object of the intellect; its cultivation then lies in fitting it to apprehend and contemplate truth'. Newman also warns against 'the philosophy of Utility', an approach that restricts education to what can be 'weighed and measured'.

And for those who argue education must be of practical use Newman argues a liberal education has 'great secular utility' as it is best able to foster the ability to critically evaluate, to think rationally and to be culturally literate.

The English poet T. S. Eliot argues in a similar vein when he suggests universities 'should stand for the preservation of learning, for the pursuit of truth, and in so far as men are capable of it, the attainment of wisdom'.

While now most likely condemned for his 'whiteness' and guilty of 'Western supremacism' the English philosopher Michael Oakeshott also suggests a university education should never be restricted to what is utilitarian or immediately contemporary and relevant.

The purpose of a university education is to enable students 'to recognise the varieties of human utterance and to participate in the conversation they compose'.

As noted by the Australian author Don Markwell in *A Large and Liberal Education* Australia's early universities established in Sydney and Melbourne championed a liberal education and one very much in the tradition of Oxford and Cambridge.

Those responsible valued 'the importance of a university embracing a wide range of subjects, including the traditional liberal arts, with students being exposed to that breadth of human knowledge'. And for most of 19th and 20th centuries as noted by the NSW academic Alan Barcan in *Sociological Theory and Educational Reality* this liberal view of education prevailed.

Fast forward to more recent times and it's obvious as argued by the sinologist Pierre Ryckmans a liberal view of education has been replaced by a cultural-left, ideological view drawing on a rainbow alliance of radical neo-Marxist, gender and sexuality, postmodern, feminist and post-colonial theories.

Academics opposed to the prevailing cultural-left orthodoxy and group think are shunned, have little chance of promotion or of receiving research funding and being published in peer reviewed journals. Such is the prevalence of identity politics and a culture of victimhood that trigger warnings, safe spaces and diversity toolkits are commonplace.

Classic literature is reduced to deconstructing texts in terms of power relationships and Western civilisation condemned as promoting 'racism, sexism, classism, historical injustice and prejudice based on religion'.

Even the once great University of Sydney has succumbed. In language much like that of Orwell's Big Brother the purpose of education is to 'unlearn'. Students have to be taught to 'challenge the established, demolish social norms' in areas such as same-sex marriage, Indigenous land rights, peace studies, refugees and the environment.

What's to be done? While it is impossible to repeat the past there are positive signs. Sydney's liberal-arts Campion College represents a beacon of sanity. Western civilisation programs funded by the Institute of Public Affairs, the Mankall Economic Foundation and the Ramsay Centre for Western Civilisation also suggest not all is lost.

There is also the essential truth that human nature is such that cultural-left ideology and group think represents a very thin and disappointing gruel that pales into insignificance given the enduring, rich and enlivening heritage offered by the great works of Western culture embodied in a liberal education.

Faith is the key for the covid blues

The Conservative Woman
20 August 2020

There's no doubt as a result of the COVID-19 virus and its debilitating and destructive effect on society both medically and economically that increasing numbers of people are distraught and in danger of suffering anxiety, loss and depression.

Whether measured by alcohol consumption, family violence, calls to organisations like Beyond Blue or the incidents of self-harm and in extreme cases suicide it's clear the fabric that holds communities and families together is under threat.

What's to be done? As someone who grew up in a violent and dysfunctional house with a drunken, violent father who deserted his family and left them destitute I'm the first to admit there is no easy answer.

The consequences of being evicted, the knowledge as a young boy you could never protect your mother and the sense that life was falling apart all conspired to instil a sense of hopelessness and despair.

As such I can empathise with those who have lost their jobs, who face bankruptcy and those whose aspirations and hopes for the future have been dashed because of an apparently random event never expected and outside their control.

While many argue we now live in a secular, post Christian age as a young boy raised as a Catholic what Jesus had to suffer epitomised by the

Stations of the Cross taught me suffering and pain are inevitable aspects of life.

This world is not a utopia and to be human is to have to confront and deal with setbacks and events that conspire to unsettle and destroy. With God's love and grace it is possible to find comfort and reassurance.

As stated by St Teresa of Avila 'Let nothing disturb thee, Nothing affright thee; All things are passing, God never changeth!'. The English Christian mystic Julien of Norwich expresses the same sentiment when she writes 'All shall be well, and all shall be well and all manner of thing shall be well'.

While this is a very different time it's also vital to learn from those involved in the Pacific War we recently celebrated. The 75th anniversary of the war in the Pacific signalled a dark and harrowing period where Australia faced the prospect of imminent invasion and defeat.

On the home front people experienced a strong sense of patriotism and allegiance to the nation as well as loyalty and commitment to family and friends. While today's society is characterised by divisive and competing interests it's time to reassert that we are all Australians regardless of class, gender, ethnicity or the colour of one's skin.

Reading about and listening to those who experienced the evil and barbarous treatment in Singapore's Changi Prison or on the Burma Railway and the Sandakan death marches it's also good to remind ourselves of how fortunate we are by comparison.

We have never been made to suffer the starvation, disease and cruelty experienced on a daily basis by those captured by the Japanese. We have never suffered the trauma and anguish suffered by those seeing their mates starved and beaten to death and knowing they were powerless to act.

Whether billion-dollar government interventions like Job Keeper and the Job Seeker additional payment or the philanthropic work of Christian organisations like the Salvation Army and Mission Australia there is a safety net to help those in need.

Those men and women who suffered the gruelling privations and dangers of the pacific war when asked talk about the value of mateship and the support of loved ones. Previous generations also were taught they must fight on and not give up regardless of the odds and how dire the situation.

While human traits like courage, optimism and resilience are increasingly lacking in today's world of self-gratification and materialism it's obvious older generations believed in something more enduring and life affirming that gave them the ability to cope with adversity and loss.

When our son, James, was killed in a hit and run accident we were left shell shocked and devastated searching endlessly for the reason he was so cruelly taken. His school chaplain comforted us with the belief even though evil exists and we cannot control our fate or the fate of loved ones there is comfort.

As stated by Julian of Norwich 'If there is anywhere on earth a lover of God who is always kept safe, I know nothing of it, for it was not shown to me. But this was shown: that in falling and rising again we are always kept in that same precious love.'

It's rare that anyone gets through life untouched by loss, sorrow and grief. The challenge has always been and will continue to be how we deal with and cope with the inevitable pain and suffering.

Unto them a child is born: the joylessness of secular faiths

Spectator Australia
20 December 2020

While those committed to extreme forms of secularism argue religion, especially Christianity, must be abolished it's ironic that at the same time they adopt many of the characteristics of the very belief systems they wish to destroy. Secularism becomes a new religion.

As to the explanation, one reason offered by Adam Zamoyski in his book *Holy Madness* tracing the impact of the Enlightenment and radical forms of humanism is because abolishing religion, especially Christianity, results in a spiritual and moral vacuum yearning to be filled.

Drawing on the example of the French Revolution (1789-1799) Zamoyski writes 'Man seeks ecstasy and transcendence, and if he cannot find them in church, he will look for them elsewhere'. Denying faith in God also leads citizens pledging allegiance to various secular inspired political philosophies and movements dedicated to 'constructing heaven on earth'.

In the same way, the Christian faith draws on a text central to its teachings so too do revolutionary movements such as socialism and communism define themselves in terms of a seminal text considered paramount. While Christians worship the Bible revolutionaries praise Das Kapital and Karl Marx.

Christian martyrs and saints are lauded and worshipped for doing God's work and for often suffering torture and death as a result. Figures like Sir Thomas Moore and more recently Australia's Saint Mary MacKillop inspire dedication and faith in others.

Revolutionary movements also have their iconic heroes including Lenin, Stalin, Mao, Ho Chi Minh, Castro and Che Guevara plus martyrs including America's anarchists unfairly convicted for committing robbery, Nicola Sacco and Bartolomeo Vanzetti, plus Black Lives Matter's George Floyd.

Throughout history, various religions have warned about an impending apocalypse where sinners are told unless they repent the world will be destroyed. Those preaching the evils of man-made global warming, as well as worshipping the teenage prophet Greta Thunberg, also predict the world's end unless the planet becomes carbon neutral by 2030.

Some religious sects are so doctrinaire and authoritarian that any who question or fail to conform are declared heretics and either banished or punished. In communist Russia under Stalin and during Mao's reign in China any who deviated from the party line or who questioned the Great Leader experienced a similar fate either ending up in death camps or being expunged from history.

While less extreme, today's cultural-left ideologues, including those committed to gender fluidity, man-made climate change and identity politics are also doctrinaire, intolerant and rigid with anyone failing to conform vilified and attacked. One either succumbs to the prevailing groupthink or is ostracised and silenced.

Notwithstanding the similarities it's clear extreme secularism, while adopting a number of characteristics associated with religion, is the polar opposite. While Jesus in the New Testament preaches non-violence epitomised by the statement 'Blessed are the peacemakers: for they shall be called the children of God' movements like communism are inherently violent.

As noted by Pope John Paul 11: 'When people think they possess the secret of a perfect organization that makes evil impossible, they also think they can use any means, including violence and deceit, in order to bring that organization into being. Politics then becomes a 'secular religion' which operates under the illusion if creating paradise in this world'.

Lenin's statement 'Not a single problem of the class struggle has ever been solved in history except by violence' and Mao's aphorism 'political power grows out of the barrel of a gun' illustrate an essential difference. As outlined in *The Black Book of Communism* the brutal reality is communism, instead of salvation, has led to the death and suffering of countless millions.

As detailed by Larry Siedentop in *Inventing the Individual The Origins of Western Liberalism* Christianity is based on concepts like the inherent dignity of the person, free will and individual agency, the presence of good and evil, promoting social justice and a commitment to the common good.

Totalitarian ideologies, on the other hand, justify cruelty and violence by arguing the end justifies the means and whatever must be done to further the revolution is allowed. Instead of free will Antonio Gramsci's concept of cultural hegemony, where the capitalist state manipulates and controls, denies individual agency as citizens are conditioned by larger historical and economic forces outside their control.

As noted by Zamoyski, radical secular movements and philosophies, unlike Christianity, also deny a spiritual, aesthetic and transcendent sense of life. Art, music, literature and dance, instead of dealing with the sublime, are part of the capitalist state's superstructure complicit in oppressing and subjugating the lower classes.

Whereas Christian England and Europe are responsible for Bunyan's *Pilgrim's Progress*, Dante's *Divine Comedy*, Michelangelo's *Sistine Chapel*, Chartres Cathedral and Beethoven's *Missa Solemnis* one searches in vain for anything comparable arising from communist Russia, China or North Korea.

You don't win if you don't fight—defend cultural conservatism and its Christian underpinnings

Quadrant Online
15 September 2021

The late philosopher and cultural critic Roger Scruton in his book *Conservatism* details the emergence of what he describes as 'cultural conservatism'. Scruton defines this as an intellectual movement centred on 'exploring the roots of secular government in the Christian inheritance, and the place of religion in a society which has made freedom of conscience into one of its ruling principles'.

In response to disparate threats ranging from fundamentalist Islam and totalitarian communism to free market neo-liberalism and neo-Marxist inspired political correctness Scruton argues cultural conservatives seek to re-establish 'confidence not in our political institutions only, but in the spiritual inheritance on which they ultimately rest'.

The freedom and liberties we take for granted have not arisen accidently or spontaneously but have evolved over thousands of years and are unique to Western civilisation. The price for freedom is eternal vigilance and unless acknowledged and defended what is most valuable soon disappears.

Such are the threats to the West's freedoms and way of life Scruton counsels 'We must rediscover what we are and what we stand for and having rediscovered it, be prepared to fight for it. That is now, as it has ever been, the conservative message'.

Proven by recent events it's clear Australia, in addition to being threatened by external forces including fundamentalist Islam, communist China and globalisation, is also under threat from enemies within. Enemies, who instead of acknowledging and defending our institutions and way of life, consistently attack, undermine and disparage what is most precious.

Cultural-left academics committed to postcolonial and critical race theories argue Western civilisation is racist and guilty of oppressing those considered inferior. The arrival of the First Fleet is condemned as an invasion leading to genocide and students taught to embrace diversity and difference and encouraged to see themselves as global citizens instead of proud Australians.

While the Australian national curriculum presents a black armband view of history and prioritises teaching Aboriginal and Torres Strait Islander culture and spirituality what we owe to Western civilisation, especially liberalism and Judeo-Christianity, is either belittled or ignored.

Freedom of conscience and freedom of expression are also under attack where anyone who dares question or disagree with politically correct ideology and mind control, with rare exceptions, is immediately condemned and vilified in the media and on social networking sites.

Question multiculturalism and you are xenophobic, doubt man-made global warming and you are a climate denier and argue marriage involves a man and a woman and you are heteronormative, homophobic and worst of all Christian. Like George Orwell describes in his dystopian novel *1984* those in control have weaponised language to enforce group think.

Instead of tolerating diverse views and rational debate people now lose their jobs or face being dragged before anti-discrimination commissions for simply speaking what they see as the truth. Ignored is Orwell's statement 'If liberty means anything at all, it means the right to tell people what they do not want to hear'.

As argued by America's non-binary feminist, Camille Paglia, such is the dominance of cancel culture that 'We are plunged once again into an ethical chaos where intolerance masquerades as tolerance and where individual liberty is crushed by the tyranny of the group'.

What's to be done? It's vital to call out political correctness for what it is and what it seeks to do. Political correctness, and it's most recent manifestation cancel culture, are not about ridding society of unfair discrimination, instead both are critical aspects of the cultural-left's long march to subvert and overthrow capitalism, Judeo-Christianity and Western society.

As argued by John Howard when prime minister, it's also critical for cultural conservatives to enter the public square and engage in the battle of ideas. If the field is vacated the battle is already lost.

Resisting the enemy within, while acknowledging its faults, requires defending what is most beneficial about nations like Australia. As detailed in David Kemp's books on liberalism in Australia we have inherited a profoundly liberating and empowering political and legal system that champions popular sovereignty, equality before the law and the right to life, liberty and the pursuit of happiness.

As noted by Roger Scruton and also argued by the Perth based academic Augusto Zimmerman underpinning our political and legal institutions is the New Testament and Christian concepts like the inherent dignity of the person, the need to love thy neighbour as thyself and to promote goodness and resist evil.

While the cultural-left seeks to banish religion from the public square, arguing it has no role to play when deciding public policy and government legislation, it is also critical to point out that without a strong moral and ethical compass societies, proven by communism and fascism, soon descend into chaos and barbarism.

Faith-based schools and Christianity in the curriculum

The strengths and benefits of Catholic and Independent schools

The Conversation

14 August 2014

Two recent comment pieces published on The Conversation (Barbara Preston and Jennifer Chesters) argue that parents might be wasting their money paying for a non-government school education as government school students do better at university and, especially when compared to students from independent schools, have better labour market outcomes.

Defining the value of a school education in terms of tertiary performance and employment outcomes ignores the fact that there are many other less utilitarian reasons why parents might choose a Catholic or independent school.

The faith-based nature of many non-government schools, the fact that most have extensive co-curricula activities, including Saturday sport, and the fact that such schools have a school culture that parents identify with are also important considerations.

There is also a considerable amount of research suggesting that non-government schools, compared to many government schools, achieve stronger educational outcomes in areas like completion rates, academic results, success at the tertiary level and promoting social cohesion.

The '2013 Melbourne Institute Working Paper Series Working Paper No. 39/13' investigating the impact of Catholic schooling on wages concludes 'during the prime time of a career, wage rates for Catholic school graduates progress with labour market experience at a greater rate, on average, that wage rates for public school graduates'.

The Working Paper, after 15 to 25 years of labour market experience, puts the benefit for Catholic school graduates at 'around 12% higher growth in real hourly wages compared to wage projections for those who attended government schools'.

Francis Vella, in an earlier paper titled 'Do Catholic Schools Make a Difference?: Evidence from Australia' reaches a similar conclusion when he writes 'We also find that individuals from Catholic schools are more likely to find employment and are paid higher wages in addition to the effects operating through the higher levels of achieved education'.

In relation to tertiary studies, the first thing to note is that non-government school students, on average and even after adjusting for socioeconomic status (SES), are more successful at gaining entry as they achieve stronger Year 12 results compared to government school students.

Melbourne-based researcher Gary Marks, in *School sector and socioeconomic inequalities in university entrance in Australia: the role of the stratified curriculum*, concludes, based on his research and the research of others 'that attendance at a Catholic or independent school significantly increased the odds of university participation, net of socio-economic background and prior achievement'.

Contrary to the argument that independent school students have a higher dropout rate compared to government school students, Marks also argues in 'LSAY Research Report 51' 'students who had attended an independent school were no less likely to complete their course than students who had attended a government school'.

While, as cited by Barbara Preston, there are a number of English studies concluding that state school students, compared to non-government school students, achieve stronger tertiary results, the research is not all in agreement.

Alan Smithers, in his paper 'University Admissions School Effect and HE Achievement', after citing research in agreement with Preston's argument, states 'However, the difference is small and is not consistent. In addition, there are differences with university, the schools, the subjects studied and gender'.

A research paper by the Higher Education Funding Council for England, *Higher Education and Beyond Outcomes from full-time first degree study,* concludes that students from independent schools outperform students from government schools in terms of (1) completing a degree, (2) achieving a first or upper second and (3) gaining employment or (4) undertaking further study.

The research paper states 'The sector-adjusted averages, like the raw data, show that a greater percentage of students from independent schools can be expected to achieve each of the four outcomes than those from state schools'.

One of the criticisms often directed at non-government schools is that they undermine a commitment to the common good and lead to social fragmentation. Once again, the evidence suggests otherwise.

A second LSAY report investigating volunteering as an essential aspect of active citizenship, 'Research Report Number 32', states 'students at government schools did less volunteering (in frequency and hours) than students in either Catholic or independent schools'.

The report also cites US research showing that Catholic school students, compared to government school students, are more likely to volunteer to perform community service. Research carried out by the Canadian based Cardus think-tank also concludes that students from faith-based schools contribute in a positive way to social stability and social cohesion (see 'Cardus Education Survey 2011').

When comparing the incidence of racism in Catholic and government schools a report commissioned by the Foundation for Young Australians titled 'The Impact of Racism of the Health and Wellbeing of Young Australians' concluded that 'Those students who attend a Catholic school are 1.7 times less likely to report experiences of racism than students attending government schools.'

Religion in the state school curriculum

Eureka Street
30 August 2015

The recent Victorian government decision to remove Religious Instruction classes from the formal school curriculum, and to only allow schools to carry out classes before or after school or at lunchtime, has reignited debates about the place of religion in state-controlled schools.

On one hand *The Age* editorial supports the change when it states: 'Some 143 years after Victoria's Education Act made clear that education must be free, secular and compulsory, the Andrews government has committed to abolishing special religious instruction classes during school hours. That is as it should be'.

Rob Ward from Access Ministries, the main provider of Religious Instruction classes, on the other hand as reported in *The Age*, is quoted as disagreeing when he argues: 'The decision seems to emphasise secularism at the expense of faith'.

In relation to being secular it is true that state-based legislation forbids government schools from teaching about religion. In Victoria, for example, the Education and Training Reform Act 2006 states: 'education in government schools must be secular and not promote any particular religious practice, denomination or sect'.

The Western Australian School Education Act section 68(1a) argues in a similar vein when it states: 'curriculum and teaching in government schools is not to promote any particular religious practice, denomination or sect'.

Ignored, though, is the fact that the various state governments, while arguing that state schools should not promote one religion or belief system over another, accept that there is a place for religion in the school curriculum. Both in terms of Religious Instruction and also by being incorporated into subjects like history, literature, music and the arts.

The NSW legislation requires state schools to offer religious education classes for 'children of any religious persuasion' and the Victorian legislation requires students to be taught 'about the major forms of religious thought and expression characteristic of Australian society and other societies in the world'.

In its submission to last year's review of the Australian national curriculum, a Foundation to Year 10 curriculum currently being implemented by all the states and territories, the body responsible for designing the curriculum, the Australian Curriculum, Assessment and Reporting Authority, also argues that students have the right to be taught about 'different religions, spiritualities and ethical beliefs'.

The 'Melbourne Declaration', the road map used by the various state, territory and commonwealth education ministers when formulating education policy, also argues that Australian students, whether in government or non-government schools, need 'to understand the spiritual, moral and aesthetic dimensions of life'.

Clearly, the fact that various state-based legislation argues education in government schools, as opposed to non-government faith-based schools, should be secular in nature does not exclude Religious Instruction classes or incorporating religion in the broader curriculum.

What might this involve? In relation to the broader school curriculum many of the submissions to the national curriculum review argue that as Judeo-Christianity is one of the world's major religions, certainly in relation to its impact on Western civilisation and Australia's development as a nation, that there needs to be a greater emphasis.

The submission by the Anglican Education Commission in Sydney argues: 'Our justice, government, education, health and general welfare systems are all established on the Judeo-Christian foundation of this civilisation'.

The Catholic Education Commission of Victoria puts a similar case when arguing that the moral and ethical teachings associated with Judeo-Christianity: 'are the foundations of our liberal democracy'.

A number of other submissions, including one from Rabbi Dr Shimon Cowen, argue that as Australia is increasingly a multi-faith, multi-cultural society that students should be familiar with and understand a range of religions including but not restricted to Judeo-Christianity.

To argue that religions should have a greater place in the school curriculum is not to proselytise. Rather it is to recognise, while we are a secular society, that students need to encounter a more transcendent sense of life that incorporates a strong moral, spiritual and ethical dimension.

As argued by T. S. Eliot in *Notes Towards a Definition of Culture*, it is also the case that religion is a fundamental aspect of any culture and if students are to be culturally literate religion needs to be incorporated in the formal curriculum.

Discounting Christianity in our schools denies history

The Herald Sun
19 January 2016

With schools opening and students about to return, education is in the news. While school funding, academic standards and teacher quality are perennial issues, equally as vital is what is taught in the school curriculum.

And when it comes to the curriculum, one of the burning issues both here and overseas is the place of religion in the school day.

In his Christmas speech British Prime Minister David Cameron said Britain was a 'Christian country' and the Education Secretary, Nicky Morgan, has ordered schools to teach that 'the religious traditions of Great Britain are, in the main, Christian'.

The NSW Government argues that Special Religious Instruction classes are an essential part of the normal school curriculum and, unlike in Victoria, classes will not be banished to lunchtime or before and after school.

The Andrews Government, on the other hand, instead of recognising our Christian heritage, is pushing a secular, anti-Christian agenda. Evidence includes taking Special Religious Instruction classes out of the school timetable.

Further evidence is the decision to ban Christmas hymns that acknowledge the birth of Christ during the normal school day. While secular Christmas decorations and carols are permitted in state schools, what is described as 'praise music (that) glorifies god or a particular religious figure or deity regardless of music style' cannot be part of a normal school activity.

No doubt the same restrictions that apply to Christmas will also apply to Easter.

The Australian National Curriculum, which Victorian schools have to teach, is also secular. In history students are told at every year level that they must learn about Aboriginal and Torres Strait Islander culture, customs and spiritual values and beliefs but there are few references to Christianity.

The Civics and Citizenship curriculum, when detailing the contribution of charitable, community and philanthropic groups, makes no mention of the Brotherhood of St Lawrence, St Vincent De Paul or the Salvation Army.

Even though Christianity is a central part of Australia's history and culture, the argument is that we are a multicultural, secular society and that religion is irrelevant.

Ignored is that Australia is a Western, liberal democracy where concepts like the sanctity of life, free will, truth telling and individual rights and freedoms are largely based on the Bible, especially the New Testament.

The Preamble to the Australian Constitution includes the words 'Humbly relying on the blessing of Almighty God' and that Parliaments around Australia begin with the Lord's Prayer.

And, as detailed by the Tasmanian author, David Daintree, in his recent book, *Soul of the West: Christianity and the Great Tradition*, the reality is that Western art, literature and music are also influenced by Christianity.

Classics like *The Pilgrim's Progress, The Canterbury Tales*, Dante's *Inferno* and more recent classics like *The Chronicles of Narnia* and novels by Patrick White have a strong Christian influence. Michelangelo's *Sistine*

Chapel, da Vinci's *The Last Supper* and music like Handel's *Messiah* and songs like *Amazing Grace* only exist and have meaning because of Christianity and the Bible.

The Australian Education Union argues that 'public education is secular' and that there must be 'freedom from religion in teaching programs'. What the union ignores is that the Victorian legislation clearly states that government schools are allowed to teach 'about the major forms of religious thought and expression characteristic of Australian society and other societies in the world'.

The Melbourne Declaration is the policy document endorsed by all education ministers and it also argues for including religion in all schools when it states that a balanced education must teach moral, spiritual and aesthetic beliefs and values.

It's true Australia is a secular society with a division between church and state, but the reality is that we, like Britain, are a Christian nation where religion underpins much of who and what we are.

Religion is central to the school curriculum

Melbourne Catholic Magazine
May 2017

What is the place of religion, especially Christianity, in the school curriculum? For Catholic schools the answer is straightforward. As noted by Catholic Education Melbourne, Catholic identity is central to the work of schools on the basis that 'A Catholic education is founded on the person and teachings of Jesus Christ and invites every member of the school community to an encounter with Jesus'.

Under the heading 'Vision, Mission and Values' the statement is also made 'Each person is created in the image of God and called to communion with God. Therefore, all human life is sacred and every human being has an innate dignity. This understanding of the human person is at the heart of the values that underpin Catholic education'.

The answer is less clear in relation to government schools where the argument is often put that as state schools are secular there is no place for religion. In its submission to the 2014 Review of the Australian National Curriculum the Australian Education Union (AEU) argues against religion in government schools on the basis that:

'As part of the great education settlement in the colonies of the latter part of the nineteenth century it was agreed that public systems of education would eschew instruction of a dogmatic and specific kind. Part of the guarantee of freedom of religion in this country was to be based on freedom from religion in teaching programs'.

The Victorian Education and Training Reform Act 2006 appears to justify such a view when it states 'education in government schools must be secular and not promote any particular religious practice, denomination or sect'. A closer reading of the Act, though, suggests that teaching about religion, including Christianity, is permitted.

In addition to allowing Religious Instruction classes in government schools the Act includes the statement that state schools are expected to teach students 'about the major forms of religious thought and expression characteristic of Australian society and other societies in world'.

Clearly, if government school students are to learn about 'the major forms of religious thought and expression characteristic of Australian society' then Christianity, especially Catholicism, must be included in the curriculum.

As noted by the 2011 Australian Bureau of Statistics approximately 61% of those who responded identified as Christian (with Catholics at 25.8% and Anglicans at 17.1%) whereas Islam accounted for 2.2%, Buddhism 2.5% and Hinduism 1.3%.

An additional justification for including religion in the curriculum can be found the Melbourne Declaration which is the road-map used by education ministers to inform policy development. The declaration states that a balanced and comprehensive curriculum should enable students 'to understand the spiritual, moral and aesthetic dimensions of life'.

A 2011 research report commissioned by the Australian Human Rights Commission, titled 'Freedom of religion and belief in 21st century Australia' also concludes that religion has an important place in the school curriculum when it states 'there was a majority consensus on the need for, and benefits of, education about religion'.

While Australia is a secular society, where there is a distinction between church and state and the commonwealth cannot make laws 'for establishing any religion' or 'imposing any religious observance', it is also the case that Christianity has had, and continues to have, a significant and profound impact on our way of life.

At the time of federation 96.1% of Australian's identified as Christian, the preamble to the constitution includes the words 'Humbly relying on the blessing of Almighty God' and parliaments across Australia, with the exception of the ACT, begin with the Lord's Prayer.

The Perth-based academic, Augusto Zimmerman, when detailing the nature and origins of Australia's legal and political systems argues 'When considered alongside the development of colonial laws, the adoption of the English common-law tradition and American system of federation, it is evident that the foundations of the Australian nation, and its laws, have discernible Christian-philosophical roots'.

On tracing the evolution of concepts like inalienable rights, where all are entitled to what the *American Declaration of Independence* describes as 'life, liberty and the pursuit of happiness', Larry Siedentop in *Inventing the Individual: The Origins of Western Liberalism* also argues Christianity has had a profound and ongoing effect.

Siedentop writes: 'For Christian beliefs had begun to impinge on the traditional conception of society by the later second century. Indeed, these beliefs began to lay the foundation to a new conception of society'. As Siedentop details, the belief in the sanctity of life, free will, the dignity of the person and a commitment to the common good are essentially Christian in nature.

Christianity is also highly relevant when considering what constitutes a balanced and worthwhile curriculum given the impact the Bible, especially the New Testament, has had and continues to have on literature, art, music and architecture.

Such is the Bible's impact on English language and literature that the British atheist Richard Dawkins argues anyone unfamiliar with the King James Bible is 'verging on the barbarian'. Of interest is that Julia Gillard when Prime Minister and Tony Abbott when Leader of the Opposition both suggested that the Bible be included in the school curriculum.

The Chaucer's *Canterbury Tales*, Dante's *Divine Comedy* and more recently T S Eliot's poetry, Graham Green's works and those Dostoyevsky as well as C. S. Lewis' The Narnia series are all deeply immersed in Christianity.

Western art, including classic works like Michelangelo's *Sistine Chapel* and his sculpture *Pieta*, Da Vinci's *The Last Supper* and Caravaggio's *The Entombment of Christ* are unsurpassed masterpieces that still resonate today.

In the same way, whether Gregorian Chants, requiems by Faure and Rutter, Bach's *Mass in B Minor* or Handel's *Messiah* it is impossible to understand and appreciate Western music without some knowledge of Christianity.

Religion belongs in schools

Quadrant online
11 April 2018

Given the School Chaplaincy program is up for review in this year's federal budget it's only natural there is a debate about whether or not it should be funded. Critics, including the Australian Rationalist Society, leave no doubt as to their opinion, arguing there is no place for chaplaincy programs in government schools, as they are secular and, supposedly, because there are too many examples of chaplaincy programs pushing extreme religious views. These are depicted as 'denigrating' and 'harming' students.

The first thing to note is that there are two different programs operating in government schools around Australia and it is wrong to treat the two as equivalent. The first involves Special Religious Instruction (SRI) classes and the second involves the School Chaplaincy program.

Whereas SRI involves formal lessons with associated curriculum material, the second involves schools receiving funding to employ a chaplain to act as a counsellor and to offer students, teachers and parents social, emotional and spiritual guidance and support. Criticisms concerning alleged examples of unacceptable religious materials finding their way into schools relate to the Special Religious Instruction classes and not school chaplains.

It should also be remembered that the chaplaincy program is voluntary and that in order to receive funding there are strict guidelines that must be agreed to. Parents must give consent before their children are involved, chaplains must not preach or advocate for a religion, and they must also abide by a Code of Conduct that ensures students are not discriminated against because of their sexuality or gender or whether they are religious or not.

And while there are critics it's also true that there are many who support the continuation of the chaplaincy program. The Education Minister Simon Birmingham recently argued in a radio interview 'many schools find it a valuable additional resource', adding that 'chaplains bring a different perspective, but a very helpful one, to dealing with students in times of crisis and need.'

Contrary to the belief that because government schools are secular and there is no place for initiatives like the chaplaincy programme, or religion more generally, it also should be noted that state-based legislation allows government schools to include religion in the school day.

In Victoria and NSW, for example, legislation permits both religious instruction classes as well as students being taught about what the Victorian act describes as: 'the major forms of religious thought and expression characteristic of Australian society and other societies in the world'.

The national road map for Australian schools, the Melbourne Declaration, also suggests religion is allowed when it states that the school curriculum should address moral and spiritual values. In an increasingly materialistic, ego centred world it's vital that students understand the importance of the transcendent.

Not surprisingly the body responsible for developing the national curriculum, on which state and territory curricula are based, also suggests religion is important when arguing that students have the right 'to learn about different religions, spiritualities and ethical beliefs'.

In Western liberal democracies, such as Australia, Christianity and the Bible, especially the New Testament, underpin our way of life. So much of Western culture's literature, history, music and art are steeped in Christianity and it makes sense that students are given the opportunity to learn about what is Australia's major religion.

To argue that chaplains be allowed in government schools and that there be a greater focus on teaching about religion, either through Special Religious Instruction classes or more generally in the school curriculum, is not to preach or try to convert students. To be culturally literate and fully understand and appreciate what underpins Western civilisation students need to be familiar with the contribution and significance of Christianity.

It's also vital, given the high rates of anxiety, depression and self-harm among so many young people, that they are able to seek the help of someone in the school experienced and qualified to give support — especially at a time when students are surrounded by a 24/7 digital world involving cyberbullying, sexting and online pornography it's even more urgent that chaplains are in schools.

The Senate debate surrounding religious schools' rights show Christianity is under attack

The Daily Telegraph
4 December 2018

Yesterday's Senate debate surrounding the legislation designed to remove the right faith-based schools have over who they enrol is the most recent example of what is becoming an ever more strident secular attack against Christianity.

The debate follows a recent Senate report that argues religious schools and other educational bodies no longer have the right to 'single out certain groups for discrimination on the basis of sexual orientation, gender identity or relationship status'.

In particular, the Senate report argues the Australian government should amend the existing Sex Discrimination Act and legislate to 'prohibit discrimination against students' and to 'prohibit discrimination by faith-based educational institutions against teachers and staff'.

The mounting threat to the right faith-based schools and higher education institutions currently have to manage their own affairs according to their religious convictions, once again, highlights the broader issue of what constitutes religious freedom.

The ALP senator Penny Wong during last year's debates over same-sex marriage argued the church should not oppose gays and lesbians marrying. Wong argued that while religious freedom meant those committed to a particular faith should not be persecuted it 'does not mean imposing your beliefs on everyone else'.

Wong went on to argue that religious freedom 'emphatically does not mean deploying the power of the state to enforce one set of religious beliefs. One's own views should not determine the rights of others'.

Taken on face value such an argument, if reversed, should equally apply to the right religious bodies and organisations have to remain true to their convictions and not be forced to adopt a secular agenda that contradicts their deeply held beliefs.

Especially given, as argued by Richard Edlin in *Secularism — Australian Education's Established Religion*, that militant secularism has embraced many of the characteristics of a post-faith religion and is dedicated to reshaping Australian society in its own image.

While Wong argues for tolerance and freedom in relation to beliefs it's obvious that religious intolerance and victimisation is ever increasing.

Critics argue that those with a faith-based belief are wrong to discriminate against others and that institutions such as the Catholic Church do not have the right to act according to their moral convictions.

As a result there's no doubt that Christianity, especially Catholicism, is under attack. Whether last year's debates about same-sex marriage, legislating to allow euthanasia, removing the right faith-based schools have over how they manage themselves or sanctioning late-term abortions critics argue there is no place for religious morals and beliefs.

And the danger, of course, illustrated by past practice where the cultural-left and secular critics are rarely satisfied with their initial victory, is that after winning the first battle more demands are made and the campaign is intensified and continues on other fronts.

Denying the right which schools and tertiary bodies currently have to act according to their religious convictions in areas like enrolments and staffing is the most recent example of this campaign to undermine religious freedom and freedom of conscience and to impose a secular ideology.

The Labor Party National Platform provides further evidence of the campaign to compromise religious freedom when it argues 'no faith, no religion, no set of beliefs should ever be used as an instrument of division or exclusion, and condemning anyone, discriminating against anyone, vilifying anyone is a violation of the values we all share'.

In addition to removing the right to discriminate in relation to enrolments and employment the Labor Platform also argues all schools must adopt LGBTQI programs that address 'homophobia, transphobia and intersexphobia' and that all students must be given the right to 'express the gender they identify with, including through preferred name and dress'.

Based on events in England, where Jewish and Christian schools are being penalised by school inspectors for not implementing the government's radical LGBTQI programs, don't be surprised when religious schools here are penalised for not incorporating state mandated gender fluidity programs.

Also don't be surprised if religious schools and institutions are penalised and suffer as a result of teaching a curriculum that conforms to their beliefs and that runs counter to the cultural-left's secular ideology.

The fact that Tasmania's Archbishop Porteous was threatened to be taken before the anti-discrimination commission for distributing the 'Don't Mess with Marriage' booklet to Catholic schools portends what is to come.

The decision by Canadian law accreditation societies to deny registration to graduates from a Christian Law School because the university expects all students, including LGBTQI, to abide by its morally conservative guidelines is yet another illustration of how all pervasive the secular attack on religion will become.

Freedom of speech and freedom of conscience are defining characteristics of Western, liberal democracies — it's only right that freedom of religion is also guaranteed and protected.

Danger: the threats to Australia's Catholic Schools

The Catholic Weekly
17 June 2019

At 20 per cent of enrolments across Australia there's no doubt Catholic schools are popular with parents and their children. Based on a number of surveys its clear parents are choosing Catholic schools because they see them as providing a faith-based education; one that best reflects and supports their values and beliefs.

Such schools are also seen as providing a disciplined classroom environment, an education that addresses the whole child and one that promotes equity and excellence in education. Australian research shows, when compared to students in government schools, Catholic schools better promote tolerance and acceptance of different ethnic groups.

Research also shows that Catholic schools are helpful in strengthening what the American academic James Coleman describes as social capital. This refers to the bonds and relationships that hold communities together and that promote reciprocity and social cohesion.

Catholic schools are successful in helping students from disadvantaged backgrounds achieve strong academic results as measured by Year 12 results and tertiary entrance. After entering the workforce students who attended Catholic schools are also more likely to volunteer and to achieve financial success.

As noted by recent research carried out by Catholic Schools NSW the existence of such schools saves state and territory governments millions of dollars each and every year as students who attend such schools do not receive the same level of funding as those in government schools.

The fact that Catholic school parents pay taxes for a system they do not use while also paying schools fees, thus reducing the cost to government, means instead of being a financial burden Catholic schools represent a financial benefit to taxpayers and governments.

As argued by Dallas McInerney in a comment piece published in *The Australian*, 'Catholic school families, which already contribute to public education through their taxes, cover the additional costs through school fees that would otherwise be borne by government. Every student attending a Catholic school represents a net saving for government'.

Notwithstanding the success and benefits of Catholic schools secular critics argue funding to such schools should be reduced, supposedly, as they only serve the wealthy and privileged in society. Ignored is that the majority of Catholic schools serve low to middle class socioeconomic communities.

Another threat to Catholic schools is their ability to remain true to their faith and operate free of intrusive and unwarranted government control and intervention. In opposition to the concept of subsidiarity schools are overwhelmed with bureaucratic red tape imposed by state and commonwealth governments.

This command and control approach is a feature of governments of all political persuasions and involves tying compliance to funding in areas like national literacy and numeracy testing, teacher accreditation, implementing a national curriculum and making school performance public on the Myschool website.

One of the most serious threats to Catholic schools and their ability to remain true to their faith and the Church's teachings is the state mandated curriculum; a curriculum that adopts a deeply secular approach to education and that ignores the vital importance of Judeo-Christianity.

In the national curriculum that includes all subjects and areas of learning from the start of school to Year 10 there are literally hundreds of references to Aboriginal history, culture and spiritualty with minimal reference to Christianity and its contribution to Western civilisation and Australian society.

Ignored is that Christianity underpins our political and legal systems and that much of Western and Australian music, art and literature can only be fully understood and appreciated if one is knowledgeable about the New Testament.

Also of concern is that much of modern education adopts a postmodern relativistic and subjective view of knowledge and how individuals relate to one another and the world at large. As a result there are no absolutes or truths as knowledge is simply a social construct reinforcing the power of the ruling class.

The then Cardinal Ratzinger describes this as a situation where 'there are no grounds for our values and no solid proof or argument establishing that any one thing is better or more valid than another'.

According to such a view the Bible instead of being the word of God and inherently true is merely one text among countless others that has to be deconstructed in terms of power relationships and what has become the new trinity of gender, ethnicity and class.

Proven by the policies taken to the recent election by the Australian Labor Party and the Greens Party there is also the danger that religious freedom will be lost as Catholic schools will no longer have the right to decide who they enrol, who they employ and what they teach.

Especially in the area pf gender and sexuality, best illustrated by events in the UK where Christian schools have been penalised for not adopting the state mandated secular view, there is a distinct possibility that schools will no longer be able to teach according to their religious tenets and beliefs.

Religion and belief systems have a place in the school curriculum

The Conversation
23 March 2015

The place of religions and belief systems, especially Christianity, in the school curriculum is a sensitive issue provoking much discussion and debate in Australia.

The issue came to head in Britain last year with what has been titled the 'Trojan Horse affair'. A small number of Islamic schools were investigated about the types of values being taught. The investigations led to Prime Minister David Cameron arguing that all schools must teach what it means to be British.

Cameron has argued that Britain is essentially a Christian nation, and students should be taught values such as 'freedom, tolerance, respect for the rule of law, belief in personal and social responsibility and respect for British institutions'.

As a result of the review of the Australian national curriculum I took part in last year, the place of religions and beliefs systems, especially Australia's Judeo-Christian heritage and traditions, also became a topic of discussion and debate.

Education researcher Tony Taylor criticised the review as an example of what he termed the 'culture wars' and implied that the review's recommendations would unfairly privilege a Judeo-Christian version of religion.

In its submission to the curriculum review, the Australian Education Union warned about the danger of including the Bible in the curriculum on the basis that the establishment of state education in the late 19th century was premised on 'freedom from religion in teaching programs'.

Government schools, unlike faith-based non-government schools, are secular in nature. However, as noted in the 'Review of the Australian Curriculum Final Report', state-based legislation allows both special religious instruction classes and teaching about religion and belief systems more generally in government schools.

The Victorian legislation, for example, permits state schools to teach 'about the major forms of religious thought and expression characteristic of Australian society and other societies in the world'.

The Western Australian legislation, in addition to stating that state schools must not promote 'any particular religious practice, denomination or sect', does allow schools to teach 'general religious education'.

The 'Melbourne Declaration on Educational Goals for Young Australians' (a key policy document referred to by education ministers) is quite specific in arguing that a well-balanced and well-rounded education should deal with the 'moral, spiritual and aesthetic development and wellbeing of young Australians'.

Many of the submissions to the national curriculum review also put a strong case for including teaching about religions and beliefs systems, especially Christianity. The body responsible for the national curriculum, the Australian Curriculum, Assessment and Reporting Authority (ACARA), agrees that a national curriculum should encourage students 'to learn about different religions, spirituality and ethical beliefs'.

As expected, a number of submissions by religious bodies supported the teaching of religion in schools. The submission by the Catholic Education Commission of NSW puts the case that any balanced and comprehensive curriculum should deal with 'the role, both past and present, of faith traditions generally and Christianity specifically in the development of Australia.'

One approach to dealing with religions and belief systems is to design specific subjects taught over a number of years. As noted in the 'Review of the Australian Curriculum Final Report', such is the recommendation by Rabbi Shimon Cowen, who argues for a stand-alone subject provisionally titled Theology.

Such a subject, instead of focusing on what distinguishes various religions, would focus on 'common theological categories and ethical principles'. Cowen makes the point that the Abrahamic religions, including Judaism, Christianity, Islam and Buddhism, have common origins and embody similar ethical and moral values.

A second approach is to imbue subjects like art, literature, music and history with religious elements. *The Sistine Chapel* and Michelangelo's *David*, Da Vinci's *Last Supper*, Dante's *Inferno*, T.S. Eliot's poetry, Bach's *Mass in B minor*, Faure's *Requiem* and much of the history of Western civilisation can only be understood in the context of Christianity.

The above two approaches should not be confused with schools allowing religious instruction classes where students of a particular faith have the opportunity to learn more about their religion.

The justifications for giving students an appreciation, knowledge and understanding of major religions and belief systems are many. In addition to providing a well-rounded, comprehensive education, it is important, as argued in the submission by the Australian Association for Religious Education, in an increasingly multi-faith, multi-cultural Australia that students 'have knowledge and understanding of others'.

Ignorance often breeds hostility and suspicion whereas knowledge and understanding lead to tolerance and respect. Especially given the impact of September 11 and the sectarian violence in the Middle East, it makes sense that the school curriculum supports inter-faith understanding and dialogue.

While education has a practical and utilitarian purpose, it is also true that the curriculum deals with significant existential questions about the nature and purpose of life. Including religions and belief systems in the curriculum adds a much-needed transcendent element in an increasingly material, self-centred world.

In Britain, the conservative government has mandated teaching about religions, especially Christianity, in the national curriculum. ACARA is reviewing the report on the Australian national curriculum finalised last year that recommends a greater focus on moral and spiritual beliefs, especially Australia's Judeo-Christian heritage and traditions.

The Place of Religion in a Secular Curriculum

Quadrant Online
April 2015

The secular state arose for the first time in history, abandoning and excluding as mythological any divine guarantee or legitimation of the political element, and declaring God is a private question that does not belong to the public sphere or to the democratic formation of the public will.

Joseph Ratzinger, 'The Spiritual Roots of Europe:
Yesterday, Today and Tomorrow', in Ratzinger and Pera,
Without Roots: The West, Relativism, Christianity, Islam

Published in 2006, the book from which the above quotation is taken explores the increasing secularisation of the Western world and the loss of a sacred, transcendent view of life embodied by Christianity. In his essay Ratzinger (later Pope Benedict XVI) describes a modern Europe where the Christian religion is banished from the public square and where there is a widespread inability or unwillingness, in part, because of postmodern theory, to make judgments of relative worth.

Anthony O'Hear ('Religion and Public Life', *Quadrant*, March 2015) also explores the intersection between religion and the state, with a particular focus on Christianity. While accepting that the state has a role to play as it provides a 'framework in which people can lead peaceful and orderly lives', O'Hear, like Ratzinger, warns against what he describes as the rise of 'aggressively strident official secularism'. He provides the state's increasing influence on education, illustrated by the British national curriculum and national testing, as an example of this imbalance. Additional examples, representing what O'Hear describes as 'the illiberal abuse of state power', involve the Conservative government forcing schools to teach gay rights and admonishing Jewish and Christian schools for failing to teach the officially endorsed line concerning homosexuality and multiculturalism.

Such is the strident nature of the British government's campaign to enforce state-sanctioned thinking that Durham Free School, a Christian faith-based school, is being forced to close because of an adverse report by school inspectors. According to the inspectors, and based on a small number of children being unfamiliar with Islam, the school, supposedly, is guilty of 'failing to prepare students for life in modern Britain. Some students hold discriminatory views of other people who have different faiths, values or beliefs from themselves.'

In opposition to what is described as 'an over-mighty and illiberal state power', O'Hear advocates 'a pluralist view of society in which religion has a role to play distinct from that of the secular power or sovereign'. Much of his critique also applies to Australia, where school education has become an instrument employed by secular critics to undermine the contribution of Christianity to the nation's history and the ability of faith-based schools to remain financially viable and true to their mission.

Cardinal George Pell ('Religious Freedom in an Age of Militant Secularism', Quadrant, October 2013) warns against government authorities and secular organisations imposing 'a particular worldview' on religious institutions and individuals. In relation to faith-based schools, of which the overwhelming majority in Australia are Catholic schools, organisations like the Australian Education Union have a long history of attempting to undermine such schools by restricting funding and imposing a cultural-Left agenda.

Australia has a tripartite system of education, involving government, independent and faith-based schools, where 20 per cent of students are enrolled in Catholic schools. Religious schools, as well as non-government schools in general, receive funding from state and Commonwealth governments and there is a consensus among the major political parties and the Australian community that such schools should be supported. Not so the Australian Education Union (AEU), which argues: 'Although substantial government funding to private schools has become entrenched in Australia in recent decades, we believe there is no pre-existing, pre-determined entitlement to public funding; i.e. there is no a priori justification for public funding to private schools.'

Article 5.1 (b) of the 'UN Convention Against Discrimination in Education' states that parents should be free to choose a school that best embodies their religious beliefs and that the religious and moral education their children receive should be 'in conformity with their own convictions'. Implied in such a declaration is the belief that parents should not be financially penalised for choosing religious schools.

As argued by O'Hear, the freedom to choose is especially relevant in the context of a liberal, democratic society on the basis that 'no one has such a comprehensive monopoly of wisdom as to have the right to impose that view on everyone else'.

In addition to seeking to jeopardise the financial viability of non-government schools, the AEU, like the Australian Greens, argues that religious schools should no longer be able to discriminate in relation to who they employ. Such critics also argue that faith-based schools should have non-discriminatory enrolment policies.

In its submission to the Commonwealth's review of anti-discrimination laws the AEU argues: 'An exception for religious organisations which would enable them to discriminate on the basis of sexual orientation or gender identity should not be included in the consolidated Act.' The Greens in Victoria argue in a similar fashion in their policy on 'Sexual Orientation and Gender Identity' that its aim is to 'Amend the Equal Opportunity Act 2010 to remove exemptions for religious organisations to discriminate on the grounds of sexual orientation or gender identity'.

The policy taken to the last Victorian state election by the now Labor government mirrors the AEU and the Greens policies: 'A Labor Government will amend the 'Equal Opportunity Act 2010' and limit the 'bona fide occupational requirement' which makes it easier for employers to discriminate against people based on their sexuality.'

The AEU also argues that the school curriculum should be secular in nature and that it is wrong to assume that students, during the course of their compulsory curriculum, should be familiar with the Bible. The AEU's submission to the Commonwealth review of the national curriculum carried out in 2014 argues that the Bible has no place in the curriculum: 'One need only glance overseas to discover what unfolds when the overly zealous seek to impose the teaching of a holy book as a mandated element of a school curriculum.'

Not only is the assertion that knowledge of the Bible will lead to sectarian discord unproven, the AEU also ignores existing state government legislation that allows both non-government and government schools to include teaching about religion, and by implication the Bible, in their curriculum.

It is true that the West Australian legislation states that the 'curriculum and teaching in government schools is not to promote any particular religious practice, denomination or sect'. At the same time that legislation states that such a clause should not 'be read as preventing — (a) the inclusion of general religious education in the curriculum of a school; or (b) prayers, songs and other material based on religious, spiritual or moral values being used in a school activity as part of general religious education'. The Victorian legislation also allows schools to include teaching about religion, when it states that it is permissible to teach students 'about the major forms of religious thought and expression characteristic of Australian society and other societies in the world'.

Given that Christianity is Australia's dominant religion, both in terms of its historical and cultural significance and according to the census figures, it would seem only logical that it, along with the Bible, be included in the curriculum. Two Australian prime ministers from both major political parties, Tony Abbott and Julia Gillard, have publicly argued for the Bible's inclusion in the school curriculum. As well as having such a profound religious significance, the Bible also has an enduring and significant impact on literature, and parables like the Good Samaritan, David and Goliath, and the Lost Sheep convey in a succinct and powerful way important moral and spiritual lessons. Contemporary expressions such as 'turn the other cheek', 'an eye for an eye' and 'to cast pearls before swine' are biblical in origin and are an essential element of what the US academic E.D. Hirsch describes as cultural literacy.

All Australian states and territories are in the process of implementing a national curriculum across foundation to Year 10 in eight learning areas, including history, English, and civics and citizenship. An analysis of how religion, especially Christianity, is dealt with in the national curriculum provides further evidence of increasing secularism.

An early draft of the civics and citizenship curriculum (dated October 2012) describes Australia as a 'multicultural, secular society with a multi-faith population'. In fact Australia is predominantly a Christian nation. The nation's political and legal institutions and much of its history and culture can only be fully understood in the context of Christianity. It is not by accident that parliaments around Australia begin with the Lord's Prayer and the preamble to the Constitution includes the words 'humbly relying on the blessings of almighty God'. Significant events like Christmas and Easter, notwithstanding an increasingly overtly secular and commercial focus, are undeniably Christian in origin and can only be fully understood and valued in terms of their biblical origins.

In defining what it means to be an Australian citizen, the curriculum document goes on to say: 'Individuals may identify with multiple 'citizenships' at any one point in time and over a period of time. Citizenship means different things to people at different times and depending on personal perspectives, their social situation and where they live. This is reflected in multiple definitions of citizenship that reflect personal, social, spatial and temporal dimensions of citizenship.'

Under such a subjective, relativistic definition it appears impossible to state with any certainty what it means to be an Australian. It also runs counter to the pledge taken during the nation's citizenship ceremony: 'From this time forward, under God, I pledge my loyalty to Australia and its people, whose democratic beliefs I share, whose rights and liberties I respect, and whose laws I will uphold and obey' (version two of the pledge removes reference to God).

A commitment to democratic beliefs and rights and liberties such as freedom of religion, freedom of expression, a Westminster form of government, being innocent until proven guilty, habeas corpus, the separation of powers, property rights and a commitment to the common good (to name a few) suggest a particular definition of citizenship — one not open to multiple definitions based on personal perspectives and different 'spatial and temporal dimensions'.

It also needs to be realised that no matter how much those Australians fighting for Islamic State in Iraq or on our own soil might believe in the concept of multiple definitions of citizenship, by engaging in terrorism they have forfeited, morally if not legally, their right to being Australian.

The October 2012 version of the civics curriculum does refer to religion when it states that students should have some knowledge of the contribution made by major religions and belief systems 'to civic life and to the development of Australian civic identity'. Unfortunately, the May 2013 version of the curriculum removes any reference to religion's contribution to civic life and civic identity and, once again, there is no reference to Christianity on the basis that Australia is a secular nation 'with a dynamic, multicultural and multi-faith society'.

Based on the Consultation Report, dated November 2012, it appears that the reason for the above change was that those consulted about the October 2012 version felt that religion was over-emphasised and, as a result, there had to be 'more reference to non-religious views' on the basis that 'Australia is a secular society'.

The May 2013 civics curriculum mandates that all Australian students learn about 'cultural or religious groups to which Australians of Asian heritage belong' and 'the unique identities of Aboriginal and Torres Strait Islander peoples'. According to the writers of the national curriculum, while it is permissible to make students learn about Asian and Indigenous culture and religious customs and beliefs the same cannot be said for Christianity and Australia's Judeo-Christian heritage and spirituality.

The way history is dealt with in the national curriculum also undervalues the central importance of religion, especially Christianity, in the nation's history and the development of Western civilisation. One example relates to an early draft where those responsible replaced BC and AD with neutral terms like BP (Before Present) and CE (Common Era).

More egregious examples of how the Australian curriculum undervalues Christianity is the 2010 history syllabus where Christian is mentioned only once — but only in the context of studying other religions such as Hinduism, Buddhism, Shinto, Judaism and Islam. The 2011 history draft also illustrates an unwillingness to acknowledge the significance of Christianity to Australian culture when, under the heading of celebrations, Christmas is merely listed alongside Chinese New Year, Diwali, Hanukkah, the Moon Festival and Ramadan.

The final edition of the history curriculum, dated February 2014, continues to undermine the impact of Christianity on Western civilisation. On referring to the trans-Atlantic slave trade no mention is made of the fact that many of those responsible for abolishing slavery under British law were committed Christians. When detailing the impact of British and European settlement on Australia's Indigenous population, while reference is made to lack of citizenship, the Stolen Generations and the struggle for land rights, no mention is made of the positive impact of early Christian missions in areas like education and health.

Ratzinger and Pera, in *Without Roots*, bemoan the impact of cultural relativism and the unwillingness of many in the academy to defend Western civilisation and the significance of Christianity. Marcello Pera writes:

> *Various names have been given to this school today: post-enlightenment thinking; post-modernism, 'weak thought', deconstruction. The labels have changed, but the target is always the same: to proclaim that there are no grounds for our values and no solid proof or argument establishing that any one thing is better or more valid than another.*

In relation to the national curriculum, based on the continual references in the curriculum to celebrating 'choice and diversity' (the new code for multiculturalism) and the emphasis on teaching intercultural understanding, where the implication is that all cultures are of equal worth, the underlying philosophy is one of cultural relativism.

Ironically, the only exceptions to this unwillingness to discriminate and to teach students that some beliefs and practices are right or wrong relate to the three cross-curricula priorities: studying the environment, Aborigines and Torres Strait Islanders, and Asia. These priorities are always dealt with in a constructive and positive light and students are rarely, if ever, asked to be critical.

At the start of 2014 the Commonwealth government commissioned a review of the Australian national curriculum, and a number of submissions by various faith-based organisations provide further evidence that the curriculum fails to deal adequately with religion, Christianity in particular. The Australian Association of Christian Schools, for example, argues that the history curriculum privileges a 'Secular Humanism' worldview to the exclusion of the significant role played by Judeo-Christianity in 'shaping many Australian political, legal and social institutions'.

Such has been the public debate surrounding the place of religion, including but not restricted to Christianity, in the national curriculum that the body responsible, the Australian Curriculum, Assessment and Reporting Authority, appears to be reconsidering the issue. In a draft paper to the review of the National Curriculum titled 'Learning about Religions, Spiritualities and Ethical Beliefs in the Australian Curriculum', ACARA reaffirms what it says is its support for including religion in the curriculum. The draft paper states:

> *The Australian Curriculum provides a platform for teaching*
> *about religions, spiritualities and ethical beliefs in a balanced,*
> *informed and impartial manner where both commonalities*
> *and differences are recognised and mutual respect is cultivated.*

The most recent edition of the civics and citizenship curriculum dated 18 February 2014, unlike previous versions, refers to Judeo-Christianity a number of times.

While official curriculum documents influence what happens in the classroom, textbooks also have a significant impact. Textbooks used in Australian schools like the Jacaranda *SOSE Alive 2* (2004) and Oxford University Press *Big ideas Australian curriculum history 8* (2012) display a jaundiced and superficial view of religion, especially Christianity.

The Jacaranda book, after describing those who attacked the World Trade Centre as terrorists, asks students, 'Might it also be fair to say that the Crusaders who attacked the Muslim inhabitants of Jerusalem were also terrorists?' Equating 9/11 Islamic terrorists with the early Crusaders displays a misguided and simplistic understanding of the historical circumstances surrounding the Church's desire to reclaim Jerusalem and the Holy Lands.

When describing the role of the Church in medieval times, instead of acknowledging its beneficial impact, the textbook presents a bleak and negative picture. The Catholic Church, supposedly, enforced its teachings by making people 'terrified of going to hell', a situation where 'Old people who lived alone, especially women, and people who disagreed with the Church were at great risk'. One of the role-plays students are asked to perform involves imagining 'that as a simple, God-fearing peasant, you have been told you were excommunicated' and, in relation to how the Church treated women, students are told 'mostly they did what the Church told them to do—to be obedient wives, good mothers, and caretakers of the home'. Not only is such an interpretation of the Church's impact on women, again, simplistic, it also judges social relations of the far distant past according to contemporary ideas and beliefs.

The Oxford textbook (2012) represents an improvement on the Jacaranda textbook in that it acknowledges the beneficial impact of the Church on European civilisation. It says that in medieval Europe the 'church was a positive influence on societies across Europe—providing education, caring for the sick and supporting the community'.

The welcome observation that 'Christian beliefs and values had many positive effects on daily life, architecture, the arts and the justice system' is undermined by the qualification that Christian values and beliefs 'also provided motivations for wars, and justifications for some people's prejudices and fears'. The textbook also asserts that the medieval Church worked against 'new inventions, exploration and scientific discoveries'. Those familiar with James Hannam's book *The Genesis of Science: How the Christian Middle Ages Launched the Scientific Revolution* will appreciate how misleading the Oxford textbook is.

The same kind of criticism and close scrutiny are often not applied to other religions such as Islam. The description of Islam is impartial and ignores the often violent and destructive nature of jihad. The authors write: 'caliphs, who succeeded Muhammad, continued to spread the Prophet's teachings throughout a growing Islamic empire'. The statement that 'The Ottoman Empire and Islamic faith spread from Asia into Africa and Europe, challenging the Christian belief system of medieval Europe' ignores practices such as dhimmi where non-believers were denied the right to own property, were unfairly taxed and often lived in fear of violence and expulsion from their communities and homes.

A third textbook published in 2010 and circulated to Australian schools titled *Learning from One Another: Bringing Muslim Perspectives into Australian Schools* continues to offer a misleading and one-sided view of Islam. The textbook, on asking students to explain what they associate with the word jihad and after noting 'there are no wrong answers', explains that it can refer to 'spiritual struggle' as well as 'armed fighting, often in self-defence'.

An extract taken from *The Oxford Encyclopedia of the Islamic World, Vol 2* is cited that claims the Crusades and the 'modern war on terror' are motivated by 'greed and scorn for Islam'. The book also repeats the argument that the reason many Muslim nations are 'socio-economically and educationally disadvantaged' is because of 'former colonial powers'. Ignored is the counter-argument that the fundamentalist aspects of the Muslim religion, especially sharia law, run counter to economic and scientific advancement, and the theocratic nature of Islam also restricts innovation and change.

The third textbook also presents the growth of Islam in a neutral way that ignores the violence, destruction and loss of freedom experienced by those living in the conquered lands. The impact of expansion is described as follows: 'Many of the peoples of the newly conquered regions converted to Islam. Those who did not were allowed to live peacefully and practise their faith as long as they abided by the law of the land and paid the jizya, a tax imposed on non-Muslims.' Once again, there is no reference to the suffering, financial hardship and often execution faced by those who wished to remain true to their religion.

Unlike secular critics who often attack non-denominational Christian schools for teaching creationism and conservative views about reproduction and sexuality, the authors of *Learning from One Another* counsel tolerance and respect for Islamic beliefs about such matters.

In school textbooks, any analysis of religion should be fair and impartial. In arguing for a more inclusive and comprehensive treatment of religion, especially Christianity, it is also important to distinguish between proselytising and educating students about religion and belief systems in a broader sense.

As Anthony O'Hear argued in *Quadrant*, it is important that institutions like education retain a degree of independence and freedom from state control on the basis that 'Many areas of public life should be seen as independent of politics, even producing a counter-balance to the political through the autonomous institutions spawned in and by those areas'.

Unfortunately, the recent history of school education in Britain and Australia, especially in relation to the curriculum, is one of increasing government intervention and control. As a result, instead of subjects like history, civics, geography and literature being balanced and impartial they have become politicised and are increasingly treated as instruments for implementing government policy in areas like multiculturalism and sustainability.

At the same time, given the secularisation of Western society and the impact of postmodern theory on the academy, the significance and importance of Christianity, both historically and in terms of its continuing value and importance, are being undermined and trivialised.

One solution is to defend the financial viability and curriculum autonomy of religious schools that enrol so many students across the nation and, unlike government schools, that have a uniquely faith-based mission. A second solution is to ensure that any state-mandated curriculum deals in a comprehensive, balanced and objective way with what the Melbourne Declaration (the guiding document used by education ministers when deciding policy) describes as 'the spiritual, moral and aesthetic dimensions of life'.

National syllabus fails the first test

The Australian
29 April 2021

The most egregious flaw in the revised national curriculum is the fact, while nodding in the direction of Australia as a Western liberal democracy with a Christian heritage, the history and civics curriculums embody a politically correct, cultural-left interpretation of the nation and its place in the Asia-Pacific.

Cultural relativism prevails where Australia is described as a 'multicultural, multi-faith society' where 'citizens' identity transcends geography or political borders and people have the right and responsibilities at the global level'.

At a time when identifying as an Australian citizen is paramount, schools are told one of the essential core concepts is to embrace diversity and a subjective view of citizenship — one where 'A person's sense of who they are, and conception and expression of their individuality or association with a group culture or to a state or nation, a region or the world regardless of one's citizenship status' takes priority.

In line with the international movement to decolonise the curriculum by removing or ignoring the debt owed to Western civilisation, the curriculum further entrenches a focus on Aboriginal and Torres Strait Islander history, culture and spirituality.

In the humanities and social sciences curriculum covering the years to Year 10, there are four references to Christianity but 13 to Indigenous history and culture. In the English document, instead of introducing students to the evolving literary canon associated with Western culture, there are 45-plus references to Indigenous oral tradition, languages and texts.

Even mathematics and science are not immune, with schools told to teach Aboriginal 'algebraic thinking' and 'to learn that First Nations peoples of Australia have longstanding scientific knowledge traditions'.

Mandating as one of the three cross-curriculums priorities Asia and Australia's engagement with Asia also reveals a superficial and antiseptic understanding of what students need to learn. The Years 7–10 history curriculum, while referring to China 28 times, makes no mention of communism under Mao and the destructive impacts of the Great Leap Forward and Cultural Revolution, where millions died.

Instead, students must explore the way 'transnational and intercultural collaboration supports the notion of shared and sustainable futures, (and) can reflect on how Australians can participate in the Asia region as active and informed citizens'.

The national curriculum fails the test of nation-building; students will continue to leave school culturally illiterate.

The revised national curriculum is cancel-culture on steroids

Spectator Australia Flat White
7 May 2021

The release of the revised national curriculum, once again, has sparked a debate about the study of Judeo-Christianity and Western civilisation in the school curriculum. Critics suggest describing the First Fleet and European settlement as 'genocide' and focusing too heavily on Indigenous history, culture and spirituality leads to a politically correct, one-sided curriculum.

In particular, *The Australian* newspaper's Rebecca Urban argues the curriculum places too much emphasis on Aboriginal and Torres Strait Islander perspectives to the detriment of Australia's Christian heritage and the debt owed to Western civilisation.

Urban writes 'Australia's Christian heritage has been erased from a proposed new national school curriculum' and that 'following feedback from an Aboriginal and Torres Strait Islander Education Advisory Group, it now has elevated importance and has been incorporated directly into several subjects'.

Bella d'Abrera from the Institute of Public Affairs is also critical arguing the curriculum 'would completely remove all references to Christianity, to Ancient Greece, and to the freedoms given to us through the values and institutions of Western Civilisation. This is basic knowledge that every Australian school child should be taught'.

Australia's eminent historian Geoffrey Blainey also expresses similar concerns when arguing: 'Genocide is hardly a fair and accurate word. Aboriginal people often suffered from the frontier wars but they suffered even more from the many wars fought by their own 'nations', one against the other, during thousands of years'.

Blainey also criticises the new curriculum, designed by the Australian Curriculum, Assessment and Reporting Authority, for ignoring the significance of religion, especially Christianity, and the contribution of early Greece and Rome as one of the 'mainsprings of the civilisation most Australians inherit'.

While it's true the revised curriculum nods in the direction of Christianity with the statement 'Australia is a secular nation with a culturally diverse, multi-faith society and a Christian heritage' a closer examination of the history and civics and citizenship documents proves any reference is superficial, misleading and tokenistic.

In the history years 7–10 curriculum while there are 12 references to Indigenous culture and history there are only 4 references to Christianity: two refer to Christianity in the context of studying the Vikings, one in the context of the Spanish conquistador's conquest of the Aztecs and one related to its impact, along with Islam, when studying 'significant events from the ancient world to the modern world'.

The history curriculum includes nothing about the life of Jesus, the impact of the New Testament or the gradual spread of Christianity and its impact on the evolution of Western civilisation including concepts like the inherent dignity of the person, what constitutes the good life and the nature of good and evil.

It's also the case at the Year 7 level while studying the ancient world includes 'Egypt, Greece, Rome, India and China' students can only study one civilisation out of the five as one of the two compulsory studies must include the 'First Nations Peoples of Australia'.

The Civics and Citizenship curriculum years 7–10 is equally one-sided and biased towards Indigenous history, culture and spirituality. Under rationale, while there is one reference to Australia's 'Christian heritage', the document fails to acknowledge Christianity underpins the nation's political and legal systems and that a commitment to social justice and the common good have Judeo-Christian underpinnings.

While students are told to study the Australian Constitution and our legal system in some detail there is no reference to the fact the constitution's preamble includes the phrase 'Humbly relying on the blessing of Almighty God' and parliamentary sessions begin with the Lord's Prayer.

The Civics and Citizenship curriculum, instead of acknowledging and advocating a strong sense of what it means to be an Australian citizen, also embraces a subjective definition characterised by personal identity and choice.

A situation where 'A person's sense of who they are, and conception and expression of their individuality or association with a group culture or to a state or nation, a region or the world regardless of one's citizenship status' takes priority. So much for nation-building and promoting a cohesive and a strong sense of national identity.

That the civics curriculum embraces a politically correct, centre-left view of education is also highlighted by what is included and excluded when asking students to study international agreements. The list includes the Paris Agreement, the World Heritage Convention, the Convention Relating to the Status of Refugees and the Declaration of the Rights of Indigenous Peoples.

At a time when religious freedom is under attack, Christianity is banished from the public square and the state is sponsoring neo-Marxist inspired gender and sexuality programs it's wrong to ignore international conventions related to religious freedom and the rights parents have as their children's primary moral guardians and educators.

No need to erase history

The Daily Telegraph
12 May 2021

Mark Rose, the chair of the national curriculum's committee responsible for putting Indigenous history and culture centre stage to the detriment of Western civilisation and Christianity, argues Australia is multicultural, part of Asia and that the existing school curriculum fails to 'reflect Australia's First Nations people's calls for truth-telling'.

Wrong on all accounts. Contrary to what Rose argues, the existing national curriculum is already drowning in Indigenous history and culture. As a result of being one of the three cross-curricula priorities across foundation to Year 10, there are literally hundreds of references — ranging from the impact of European settlement to the 1960 Freedom Ride and the Mabo High Court decision.

Describing the over 500 tribes with different languages and often in conflict as First Nations that existed at the time of the First Fleet is also wrong and simply a myth perpetuated by activists. A myth that steals from the European concept of nation states and is guilty of cultural appropriation.

Describing 'Indigenous social organisation systems, protocols, kinship structures, economies and enterprises' as 'sophisticated' also makes little sense compared to a civilisation that had circumnavigated the globe, and where the Bible and British common law that arrived with Captain Arthur Phillip embodied concepts like the inherent dignity of the person and the right to a fair trial.

As detailed by the First Fleet's Watkin Tench, Aboriginal culture was especially uncivilised for women. Tench wrote: 'But indeed the women are in all respects treated with savage barbarity; condemned not only to carry the children, but all other burthens, they meet in return for submission only with blows, kicks, and every other mark of brutality.'

In addition to ignoring the dark side of Aboriginal culture, the revised national curriculum also embodies what the eminent historian Geoffrey Blainey describes as a black armband view. Instead of 'truth-telling', an interpretation that presents the arrival of Europeans as entirely negative. Students are told to study the 'impact of invasion, colonisation and dispossession of lands by Europeans on the First Nations Peoples of Australia such as frontier warfare, genocide, removal from land, relocation to 'protectorates', reserves and missions'.

Ignored is that disease caused the most suffering. The national curriculum also refuses to acknowledge the reality, as argued by the Indigenous academic Anthony Dillon, that many Aborigines have benefitted from Western culture in terms of receiving a sound education, establishing successful careers and raising a family.

Such is the dominant nature of the cultural-left's campaign to prioritise Indigenous culture and rid the curriculum of white, European supremacism that even mathematics and science are not immune. In mathematics Year 7–10, there are more than 100 references to Aboriginal mathematics.

Activities include 'creating and performing addition and subtraction stories through Aboriginal and Torres Strait Islander dances to explore the relationship between addition and subtraction' and 'investigating how song, story, and/or dance of Aboriginal and Torres Strait Islander Peoples can be represented through mathematical models using combinations of two or more of the four operations'.

While Western science is responsible for putting a man on the moon and ensuring planes stay in the air, in the science curriculum, students are told the 'First Nations Australians have worked scientifically for millennia and continue to provide significant contributions to developments in science'. Students are also told the 'First Nations Peoples of Australia have longstanding scientific knowledge traditions'.

So much for the early Greek philosophers and Western science involving Newton, Marie Curie and Einstein; a science that led to steam power, the internal combustion engine, electricity and the digital revolution.

Mark Rose is also wrong to describe Australia as multicultural and part of Asia, as 77 per cent of the population identifies as Anglo-Celtic, European or Australian, with Aborigines and Torres Strait Islanders and Chinese at approximately 4 per cent each. Christianity is also the dominant religion, sitting at just under 52 per cent. While it's true Australia geographically is part of Asia, nothing will change the fact that we are a Western, liberal democracy with deep roots in Western civilisation.

Our political and legal systems are derived from the United Kingdom, our language is English, and to deny the mainstream culture's ancestry by airbrushing it from history is an example of cultural vandalism.

It's wrong that at the same time cultural-left academics and Aboriginal apologists argue the national curriculum must prioritise Indigenous culture, history and spirituality they see nothing wrong with erasing the significance and debt owed to Western civilisation and Judeo-Christianity.

Indoctrinating students with the belief that there is nothing worthwhile or beneficial about the arrival of Captain Phillip and the First Fleet is also guilty of ensuring students are culturally illiterate and most ignorant about what makes Australia one of the world's oldest, most peaceful and prosperous democracies.

Freedom of religion under attack

Not a good time to be a Catholic

Eureka Street
27 August 2014

Now is not a good time to be a Christian — especially, if you are a Catholic. Read *The Age*, *The Sydney Morning Herald*, listen to the ABC or read Irfan Yusuf's piece on Eureka Street's blog and it's obvious that the critics are on a roll.

Wendy Squire's recent comment piece in *The Age* (Taking a leap of faith? Take the blinkers off) provides a good illustration of the often vitriolic and very public campaign to tarnish religion and to undermine the beliefs of the 52% of Australians who describe themselves as Christian.

In addition to refusing to be a godmother to a close friend's baby as the ceremony was in a Catholic Church, Squire attacks the Church for unfairly indoctrinating children, for opposing her views on marriage and abortion and for condoning child abuse.

Ignored is that Christianity is one of the foundation stones on which Western civilisation is based and that the various Christian denominations and their related organisations and community bodies constitute an overwhelmingly positive and beneficial force in Australian culture and society.

There is no doubt, as Cardinal Pell and Pope Francis admit, child abuse is an offensive, horrific and evil act that destroys the innocence and faith of those who are most vulnerable.

But, to use the fact that priests have been guilty of such an unforgivable betrayal of the Church's teachings does not mean that Christianity has no value or that we should turn our backs on Christ.

Growing up in working class Broadmeadows in a Housing Commission estate with a communist father and a Catholic mother — mass on Sunday and the Eureka Youth Movement on Tuesday — taught me firsthand about two of the most influential and powerful forces of the 20th century.

My father taught me the socialist mantra of 'from each according to his ability and to each according to his needs' and my mother taught me how to recite the rosary and to follow the Stations of the Cross.

The Eureka Youth Movement taught me about Stalin's glorious revolution and how Mao heroically struggled to free his people from years of oppression, disease and starvation.

It was only years later that I read about the gulag and how Mao's cultural revolution, like Pol Pot's Year Zero, killed millions and condemned others to poverty and oppression. The reality is that communism, as pointed out by George Orwell, is an evil ideology that promises a working class paradise on earth while delivering subjugation, suffering and thought control.

Being a Catholic, on the other hand, taught me that we have a conscience and free will, that there is good and evil, that life on earth is far from perfect and that the spiritual and transcendent are equally as, if not more important, than our physical and worldly needs and aspirations.

Many of the parables and sayings I heard as a child still resonate as they portray something essential and significant about human nature. 'Turn the other cheek', 'let he without sin cast the first stone', 'as you sow, so shall you reap' and 'be a good Samaritan' offer a strong moral compass to help navigate life's dilemmas and pitfalls.

The aphorism 'And again I say unto you, It is easier for a camel to go through the eye of a needle, than for a rich man to enter into the kingdom of God' and Jesus' act in expelling the money changes from the

Temple also resonate in an age where material pursuits and gratuitous consumption are rampant.

Studying literature at university made me realise how important Christianity is to Western literature. Bunyan's *A Pilgrim's Progress*, Blake's poetry (even though he criticised organised religion), much of T. S. Eliot's poetry and novels like Dostoyevsky's *Crime and Punishment* all require an understanding of Christianity.

Listening to Bach's *Mass in B Minor* recently performed at the Melbourne Recital Centre underscored the fact that Christianity has also profoundly affected the music that is such a fundamental part of Western culture.

The great European galleries and museums also contain thousands of religious icons, paintings and sculptures that are testimonies to how religion can inspire a sense of artistic beauty associated with the transcendent and the sublime.

From a more practical perspective Christian morals and beliefs are also a prime motivating force for charitable organisations like the Salvation Army, the Brotherhood of St Laurence and Caritas Australia.

There is also no doubt that Australia's hospital and education systems would collapse if not for the presence of Christian, mainly Catholic, schools and hospitals. Catholic schools, for example, enrol approximately 20 per cent of Australian students and save taxpayers billions every year as governments do not have to enrol such students in more expensive to fund state schools.

Having lost a son killed in a hit and run accident, I can also attest that in times of great suffering, anguish and lost that religion, while never offering complete peace and understanding, offers succour and hope.

In times of darkness and despair, as suggested by the Christian mystic Julian of Norwich, there is comfort and reassurance. She writes: 'And although the battle is not won nor the pilgrimage completed, we know that we have sufficient light. This is our source of life. But we cannot escape the suffering and the sorrow: there are dark sides to life. Realism forces us to face the fact. And the same realism enables us to trust the light and life and love in which we are enfolded'.

Talking point: Cultural Left guilty of double standard over freedom of speech

The Mercury
21 November 2015

Nothing exposes the hypocrisy and double standards enforced by Australia's cultural-left thought police than the attack on Tasmania's Archbishop Porteous for simply espousing Church doctrine in relation to same-sex marriage.

Archbishop Porteous, along with the Catholic Bishops of Australia, is about to be brought before the Tasmanian Anti-Discrimination Commission for supposedly offending and humiliating transgender Greens candidate Martine Delany.

In the booklet 'Don't Mess with Marriage' distributed to Catholic schools the Church leaders argue, while same sex couples 'must be treated with respect, sensitivity and love', that the sacrament of marriage can only involve a man and a women.

Delany argues that the Church's conviction that marriage involves heterosexuals is humiliating, offensive and insulting and Archbishop Porteous must be penalised and forced to recant.

Forget about being an open, liberal, democratic society where freedom of religion and freedom of speech are central to our way of life — the minute anyone questions politically correct doctrine they are vilified and silenced.

Even worse, it's also true that Australia's cultural-left establishment has one rule for those being attacked, like Archbishop Porteous, and another rule for itself.

Compare the Archbishop's treatment and the way Australia's PC brigade defends the right of Muslim students at a Melbourne primary school to be excused from singing Advance Australia Fair.

In a comment piece titled 'Freedom to not sing the national anthem', left-leaning Ben Pobjie argues we must defend 'the marvellous concept of freedom of religion. That's that beautiful principle that says everyone in our society can practise whatever religion they choose, or no religion at all'.

Even though Muslim Imams argue there is nothing wrong with the children singing the national anthem Pobjie goes on to argue that they should be excused 'even if the rest of us see no need for such traditions'.

Jason Wilson from the left leaning *The Guardian* argues those who believe singing the anthem should be compulsory are whipping up 'a false crisis of loyalty' and that the children should be excused as we need to promote 'perspective, hospitality and trust'.

Add the fact that ALP and Green senators recently defeated a motion moved by Tasmania's Senator Abetz supporting the democratic right of the Catholic Church to distribute the booklet and it's clear that our freedoms are at risk.

If those on the left are serious about defending freedom of religion and the inherent right we all have to enter the public debate and to advocate what we hold to be true then they would be defending Archbishop Porteous — instead, they seek to silence him.

Ignored is that the 'International Covenant on Civil and Political Rights' that Australia has endorsed argues 'Everyone shall have the right to freedom of thought, conscience and religion' and the right to manifest such a 'religion or belief in worship, observance, practice and teaching'.

As noted by the recently published *The Human Freedom Index*, it is also true that one of the most important freedoms that distinguishes free and open societies like Australia from totalitarian regimes is freedom of religion and freedom of expression.

A second example of the cultural-left's hypocrisy is its advocacy of the Safe Schools Coalition that is dedicated to 'helping schools be safer and more inclusive for same sex attracted, intersex and gender diverse students'.

The program, supported by state and commonwealth governments, seeks to create school environments that are 'free of homophobic and transphobic bullying' by providing support and resources that normalise LGBTIQ relationships.

Students are told that there is nothing unique or special about heterosexual relationships and that 'Australian and international research shows that it is the quality of parenting relationships that determines children's wellbeing, not their family structure'.

Another resource featured on the Safe Schools Coalition website warns about the belief that marriage involves a women and a man by arguing those holding such a belief are guilty of being heteronormative.

That is, being guilty of imposing 'a hierarchy where attitudes and practices that affirm heterosexuality are seen as better than those that don't. For example, believing that marriage should only be between a man and a women is a heteronormative view'.

Clearly, those seeking to condemn and punish Archbishop Porteous for communicating the Church's views about marriage while giving the Safe Schools Coalition the freedom to promote its agenda in schools have never read George Orwell's *1984*.

In the novel Orwell describes a totalitarian society where all are subjugated and forced to follow the Party line. One of the methods used to enforce compliance is doublethink – defined as 'the power of holding two contradictory beliefs in one's mind simultaneously and accepting both of them'.

If the Safe Schools Coalition is free to advocate the cultural-left's view of marriage promoted by the LGBTIQ rainbow alliance then it is both irrational and unjust to deny the same right the Catholic Church has to advocate an opposing view.

Placating evil is not tolerance

The Daily Telegraph
8 July 2016

Tim Soutphommasane, Australia's Race Discrimination Commissioner, argues in the Fairfax Press: 'Every member of our society should be free to live without fear of discrimination. This includes being free to practise their religion, as guaranteed by section 116 of the Constitution'.

Wrong. While the Constitution states 'The Commonwealth shall not make any law for establishing any religion, or for imposing any religious observance, or for prohibiting the free exercise of any religion' those responsible would not accept that all religious beliefs should be tolerated.

The reality is not all religions are peaceful and tolerant and it's clear some practices and beliefs are un-Australian.

The Hindu caste system discriminates against 'untouchables' and the system of dowry, where husbands demand money and gifts from their prospective wives' families, still leads to violence and death.

Best illustrated by Ayaan Hirsi Ali's latest book, *Heretic*, it's also true that Islamic fundamentalism is inherently violent. While arguing the majority of Muslims are 'peaceful and law-abiding' Hirsi Ali cites multiple examples of unacceptable religious practices.

Based on her own experience as a child growing up in Somalia Hirsi Ali describes the widespread practice of female genital mutilation and arranged marriages.

And her experience is not unique, according to the World Health Organisation 'More than 200 million girls and women alive today have been cut in 30 countries in Africa, the Middle East and Asia'.

In England, Prime Minister David Cameron admits '20,000 children are still at risk' and one Australian organisation suggests up to 'three girls a day are born in Australia who are at high risk'.

Hirsi Ali also writes that in Pakistan, those who blaspheme against the Prophet are 'punishable by death', in Saudi Arabia 'churches and synagogues are outlawed', in Iran 'stoning is an acceptable punishment' and in Brunei, under Sharia law, 'homosexuality is punishable by death'.

It's clear that not all religions support and protect the rights and freedoms we take for granted.

Instead of cultural relativism, so much favoured by the cultural-left, we should acknowledge that some religious practices are beyond the pale and that Western culture and Christianity are preferable.

Australia is a Western, liberal democracy, based on the Westminster system and Christianity underpins our political and legal systems. The Constitution's Preamble refers to 'Almighty God' and parliaments around Australia begin with the Lord's Prayer.

Concepts like sanctity of life, commitment to the common good, the separation of Church and state and free will owe as much to the New Testament as to the Enlightenment and political philosophers like John Stuart Mill.

And while there is no doubt that Western culture and Christianity are far from perfect, as argued by Arthur M Schlesinger, 'The crimes committed by the West have produced their own antidotes. They have produced great movements to end slavery, to raise the status of women, to abolish torture, to combat racism, and to advance personal liberty and human rights'.

Andrew's Bill puts religious freedom at risk

The Herald Sun
5 September 2016

The Andrews Government's legislation currently before parliament to change Victoria's equal opportunity act represents a significant and far-reaching attack on religious bodies and schools.

At the moment faith-based schools and bodies have the freedom to ensure whoever they employ supports their religious beliefs. While respecting privacy, religious bodies are also able to require that employees do not undermine the religious teachings that such organisations are committed to uphold.

If passed by parliament the "Equal Opportunity Amendment (Religious Exceptions) Bill 2016' will mortally weaken this freedom by opening religious schools and bodies to litigation and penalties if they discriminate against someone because of religious beliefs or activities, sex, sexual orientation, marital status, parental status or gender identity.

The attack on religious freedom will mean that Catholic and Independent schools, that enrol over 36 per cent of students and are increasingly popular with parents, will lose the right they have to decide who they employ.

Faith-based schools are not like secular, government schools. Catholic schools, for example, by their very nature are required to follow the teachings of the Church and to imbue the curriculum and a school's ethos with the word of God.

As noted in a paper written by the Catholic Bishop's Conference 'All those who choose to work in a religious organisation have a significant responsibility to maintain the religious integrity of the organisation'.

Nobody forces individuals to work in religious bodies or schools but if they do, as argued by the Bishops, it is vital that 'those who choose to work in them do not compromise or injure by word or action those religious and moral principles from which the agencies derive their foundational beliefs'.

Forcing Christian schools to employ an atheist who does not believe in God and who denigrates the Bible and denies the resurrection of Christ strikes at the very heart of why such schools exist in the first place.

Given that Christian, Jewish and Islamic religions all define marriage as involving a man and a women for the purpose of procreation it would also be wrong to force such schools to employ an LGBTI activist who was publicly campaigning for same-sex marriage.

The Australian Human Rights Commission's 2008 report titled 'Freedom of Religion and Belief in the 21st Century' agrees when it argues, 'Preference for employment for a person holding a particular religious or other belief will not amount to discrimination if established to be a genuine occupational qualification'.

This is apart from the fact that teaching is a collegiate affair and the most effective schools are those where there is a common agreement on the culture and mission of the school.

Freedom of religion is one of the basic tenets of Western, liberal democracies and it is guaranteed by state and international covenants and agreements. Such agreements also protect the right of parents to choose a school that ensures the 'religious and moral education of their children is in conformity with their own convictions'.

Those parents seeking a religious education for their children have every right to expect that the teachers employed, the curriculum and the broader school environment accord with the moral and ethical teachings of their particular faith.

One of the arguments in favour of stopping religious bodies from being able to discriminate when it comes to employment is that the individual's rights must be given priority.

The reality is that matters are not that simple. As common sense suggests, not all rights are absolute and there are occasions when particular rights have to be curtailed or qualified.

The Victorian 'Charter of Rights and Responsibilities Act 2006' accepts this is the case when it states 'there may be some cases where competing rights need to be appropriately balanced. The intention of the exceptions is to strike a balance between the rights and freedoms of individuals'.

In any community the challenge is always to balance an individual's rights against those of other individuals, society in general and the rights of community groups and organisations.

For example, feminists are happy to accept the fact that men should not be allowed to join women's only gyms and that there must be gender quotas for political parties on the basis that there should be positive discrimination for women. There are also co-educational schools that are permitted to restrict boys enrolling on the basis there are not enough girls.

The most concerning aspect of the Andrews Government's decision to change the equal opportunity act and to undermine religious groups and schools is that it represents another example of the government pushing a secular, anti-religious agenda.

Coupled with the Labor Government's decision to remove Religious Education from the school curriculum and to spend additional millions on the controversial Marxist inspired LGBTI Safe Schools program it's clear why some now describe Premier Andrews as Red Dan.

Safe Schools Coalition not so safe

The Catholic Weekly
30 September 2016

The Safe Schools Coalition program, directed at government and non-government schools across Australia, promotes itself as an anti-bullying resource that supports 'sexual diversity, intersex and gender diversity in schools'.

The program's booklet *Safe schools do better* argues that the 15.7 per cent of students who identify as same sex attracted, trans-sexual or intersex face widespread discrimination and bullying that must be addressed.

While all agree there is no room for bullying or unfair discrimination in schools the reality is the Safe Schools program, instead of being an anti-bullying resource, is more about indoctrinating students with a radical, Marxist inspired sexuality and gender agenda.

One of the chief architects of the Safe School program, Roz Ward from La Trobe University, at a professional development session for teachers admits as much when she says, 'Safe Schools Coalition is about supporting gender and sexual diversity… not about stopping bullying, about gender and sexual diversity, about same sex attraction, about being transgender, about being lesbian, gay, bisexual'.

At a 2015 Marxism Conference Roz Ward also reveals the program's radical, cultural-left agenda when she says, 'Marxism offers both the hope and the strategy needed to create a world where human sexuality, gender and how we relate to our bodies can blossom in extraordinary new and amazing ways'.

Ward goes on to argue that 'It will be through a revitalised class struggle and revolutionary change that we can hope for the liberation of LGBTI (lesbian, gay, bisexual, transgender or intersex) people' and that 'LGBTI liberation is bound together with the liberation of the whole of society and the basis for that liberation is class struggle'.

The ideology underpinning the Safe Schools program is described as 'gender theory' and is based on the belief that one's gender, instead of being biologically determined, is a social construct. Gender theory advocates argue that there is nothing preferable or normal about being a male or a female and that those who think so are guilty of 'heterosexism'.

The program, being used in over 500 state and territory schools, tells primary and secondary school students that gender is fluid and limitless, there are no boundaries, and they can choose for themselves whether they are LGBTI.

In the *Gender Fairy* story book, for example, primary school age children are told they can choose whether or not they are transgender as 'only you know whether you are a boy or a girl. No one can tell you'.

As a result, materials associated with the Safe Schools program tell schools that if boys self-identify as girls they should be allowed to use girls' toilets and girls' changing rooms. Schools are also told that the school curriculum must be redesigned so that it does not depict heterosexuality as preferable or more acceptable than being LGBTI.

Such is the controversial and ideological nature of the Safe Schools program that the Archbishop of Sydney, Archbishop Anthony Fisher OP, is quoted as criticising the program for enforcing 'an extreme form of the LGBTI agenda on schools'. And the archbishop is not alone in arguing the program runs counter to the Church's teachings about gender and sexuality.

In opposition to the belief that gender is fluid and that a person can self-identify as whatever gender they choose the Church argues gender is essentially binary in nature and that being male or female is essential to the concept of marriage.

In 2012 Pope Benedict XVI stated 'The Church speaks of the human being as man and woman, and asks that this order be respected'. The Pope also argues that treating gender as fluid leads to a 'self-emancipation of man from creation and the creator'.

More recently Pope Francis also strongly condemns gender theory when he states it 'denies the difference and reciprocity in nature of a man and a woman and envisages a society without sexual differences, thereby eliminating the anthropological basis of the family'.

The impact of gender theory on schools is not restricted to Australia with both the American and Polish Catholic Bishops warning against its destructive impact. The Polish Bishops in a pastoral letter condemn gender ideology as being 'strongly rooted in Marxism and neo-Marxism'.

The American Bishops also signal a warning in a 'Gender Ideology Teaching Resource' when they quote the Catechism as arguing: 'By creating the human being man and woman, God gives personal dignity equally to the one and the other. Each of them, man and woman, should acknowledge and accept his sexual identity'.

Such is the controversy surrounding the Safe Schools program that the commonwealth Minister for Education, Simon Birmingham, ordered an inquiry. As a result, with the exception of Victoria, the program is restricted to secondary schools, parents must be notified if their child's school adopts the program and they now have the right to opt-out.

At the same time the revised Safe Schools Coalition program still promotes a radical, cultural-left agenda and parents have every right to be concerned.

Foolish to dent what makes us powerful

The Herald Sun
2 January 2017

The alleged Christmas Day plot by Islamic terrorists targeting Flinders Street Station, St Paul's Cathedral and Federation Square should not come as a surprise.

Other Australian examples include the 2002 Bali bombings, the Holsworthy Barracks terror plot, the Lindt Café siege in Sydney and the murder of Curtis Cheng outside the Parramatta Police Station. Proven by the 9/11 attacks in America, the London bombings in 2005, the 2015 Paris attacks and the 2017 tragedy in Nice where a truck was driven into crowds of civilians, it's clear that fundamentalist Islam is committed to destroying Western, liberal democracies and our way of life.

And while Victoria's Premier Daniel Andrews appears incapable of connecting the dots (describing the Christmas Day plot as 'an act of evil' instead of an act of Islamic terrorism) there is no doubt that aspects of the Islamic religion are inherently violent.

As argued by David Cameron when he was Britain's prime minister 'simply denying any connection between the religion of Islam and the extremists doesn't work … it is an exercise in futility to deny that'.

Not only did Cameron argue fundamentalist Islam represented a religious threat, he also argued that England was a Christian nation and everyone should accept the rule of law, the Westminster parliamentary system and the British way of life.

The Somalian-born activist Ayaan Hirsi Ali makes a similar point to Cameron in her book *Heretic* when she argues, 'Islam is not a religion of peace'. While acknowledging the vast majority of Muslims want to coexist peacefully with others, Ali details aspects of the Koran that are a threat to Western civilisation.

Examples include the Koran's hostility to women and homosexuals and the concept of dhimmi — under which non-Muslims who have been conquered face the choice of converting to Islam, paying heavy taxes or death.

Other examples include Islamic groups like ISIS involved in genocide, murdering thousands of Christians and other nonbelievers and the terrorist group Boko Haram kidnapping and enslaving more than 200 Nigerian schoolgirls.

Coptic Christians are also being killed and their churches and cathedrals destroyed in Egypt simply because Christianity is not acceptable to Islamic extremists. In the book *111 Questions on Islam*, the point is also made that unlike the Bible, where different interpretations and disagreements are allowed, the words spoken in the Koran are directly from Allah and must not be challenged.

Those who question or insult the Koran such as the novelist Salman Rushdie are punishable by death. The governor of Jakarta, Basuki 'Ahok' Tjahaja Purnama, is currently facing trial for suggesting there is nothing in the Koran forbidding Muslims voting for a governor who is Christian.

While Western nations face an external threat represented by Islamic terrorism, there are also those within our community seeking to undermine our way of life.

Like Premier Andrews, who refuses to admit the link between terrorist acts and fundamentalist Islam, there are many in Australia's media and in our universities refusing to admit that aspects of the Koran are hostile to Western civilisation.

Islamic apologists appear on ABC radio and television and in the Fairfax Press arguing that Islam is not a threat and labelling those critical of the Koran as Islamophobic.

The book *Learning From One Another, Bringing Muslim Perspectives Into Australian Schools*, produced by the University of Melbourne, argues that Australian schools are guilty of teaching history that privileges a 'Eurocentric version of history'.

Australia's national curriculum, instead of celebrating the unique benefits of Western civilisation, argues in favour of diversity and difference (the new code for multiculturalism) and that all cultures are equal. Ignored is that all cultures are not equal and that Western liberal democracies like Australia are unique. Having inherited English common law and a Westminster form of government ensures all citizens are equal before the law and have the right to life, liberty and the pursuit of happiness.

It's no accident, according to the American-based Freedom House, that Western nations are among the freest in the world, guaranteeing liberties such as freedom of speech and religion, universal voting, the concept of innocent until proven guilty and the right to own property.

While we are a secular society, it is also true that Christian concepts like the sanctity of life, free will, seeking good instead of evil and committing to the common good are Western in nature.

By comparison countries in our region such as China, Vietnam, Cambodia, Lao PDR and Myanmar are totalitarian regimes where the freedoms we take for granted are suppressed. Unlike Islam, that has remained unchanged for hundreds of years, it is also true that Western civilisation has experienced periods of dramatic upheaval and change — including the Renaissance, the Enlightenment, the Reformation, the Industrial Revolution and the advent of the digital age.

Western nations are among the most prosperous and economically advanced, where science and technology have combined to put a man on the moon, split the atom, cure diseases and increase life expectancy to record levels. Let's acknowledge, defend and celebrate what we have achieved.

Be afraid, very afraid if you dare to believe

The Australian
15 August 2017

Archbishop Anthony Fisher is correct to argue Christian organisations and those of the faith will suffer 'harassment and coercion' if same-sex marriage is legalised and that any change represents a clear and present danger to freedom of expression and freedom of religion.

The reality, as argued by Tony Abbott, is that the postal vote to radically alter the nature of marriage is part of a politically correct campaign to undermine marriage as an institution and to further secularise society by banishing religion from the public square.

The Australian Education Union and the Australian Association for the Teaching of English have argued for more than 30 years that LGBTQI lifestyles must be normalised and, similar to the argument of the Marxist-inspired Safe Schools program, that marriage must be deconstructed as gender and sexuality are fluid and limitless. Currently, the road map for Australian schools, the Melbourne Declaration, declares all secular and faith-based schools must not discriminate in relation to gender, sexual orientation or religion when employing staff or enrolling students.

Compliance is tied to funding, and while faith-based schools are exempted under equal-opportunity acts , if the revised commonwealth marriage act takes precedence, faith-based schools will lose the freedom to act according to their religious beliefs. Such is already happening in Victoria where the Andrews government, with the support of the

AEU and the Greens, is moving to weaken the employment powers and enrolment policies of religious bodies by changing the anti-discrimination act.

The Melbourne Declaration also imposes a secular national curriculum on all schools, under which children are taught there is no difference between same-sex marriage and marriage involving a woman and a man. If same-sex marriage is legislated, there's no doubt religious schools will be forced to teach a secular view of marriage that contradicts their religious beliefs.

Events overseas also illustrate the dangers inherent in changing the marriage act. In England, two Christian schools have been threatened with closure for following the church's teachings relating to marriage instead of the government mandated approach. At one school the government inspector recommended it be censored as children as young as 10 were considered homophobic because they failed to articulate the government's policy of embracing diversity and difference regarding LGBTQI people.

In Atlanta, Canada a Christian school has been told to stop teaching parts of the Bible that oppose gay sex or it will lose funding. Contrary to what the Liberal MP and gay activist Tim Wilson argues, it's clear that changing the marriage act not only radically redefines the definition of marriage; any change also opens the flood gates to coercion, litigation and financial penalties against those who are committed to the sanctity of marriage and the inalienable right to religious freedom.

This is why I'll be saying 'no' to same-sex marriage

The Age
17 August 2017

There's no doubt that central to the concept of family is a definition of marriage involving a man and a woman for the purpose of procreation. With only minor exceptions over some hundreds of years and across all the major religions, this is how marriage has been, and continues to be, defined.

It's also true that about 98 per cent of Australians identify as heterosexual and according to the 2011 census figures only 1 per cent of Australian couples are same-sex, with surveys suggesting only a minority want same-sex marriage. There are more important issues to worry about.

We should also forget the Safe Schools' postmodern, deconstructed definition of marriage where gender and sexuality are fluid and limitless and individuals are free to choose whatever they choose to self-identify as.

No matter how much gays and lesbians might want to wish otherwise from a physiological and biological point of view, only men and women can have children. Such is the nature of conceiving and giving birth that to pretend otherwise is to deny how nature works.

To put it bluntly, gays and lesbians are physically incapable of procreation and having their own children. For them to believe otherwise is to deny the life choice they have made and to believe they should be entitled to something normally associated with biological parents.

It's also true that the ideal situation is where children are raised by their biological parents instead of conception involving a third party donating sperm or paying a surrogate mother. As any parent well knows, the intimate and unique bond between a biological parent and his or her child is primal in its force.

No wonder children conceived by donor sperm now have the legal right to discover their true parentage and less privileged countries such as Thailand and Cambodia are banning surrogacy.

Parents who have conceived naturally as a key aspect of what it means to be married also know that children require a male and a female role model if they are to fully mature and develop as young adults.

Both genetically and emotionally, and what is expected socially, men and women are different. While much has been done to promote equality of the sexes the fact is that boys need strong, male role models.

This I know from personal experience after losing a father to alcoholism and domestic violence as a young child and missing out on the love and companionship that only a father can provide.

In the same way, despite the campaign by feminists to erase gender stereotyping, young girls generally copy their mothers and express themselves in a feminine way. As a general rule, boys are more physical than girls and less emotionally demonstrative.

Forget the mantra that equality only occurs when all sexes are the same — it is possible to be equal but different.

Changing the marriage act to include same-sex couples radically redefines and alters the meaning of a sacred union that provides more than just a physical and emotional connection.

Such is the special union of body and spirit involved in a marriage between a man and a woman that it necessitates a unique ritual and sacred compact that should not be weakened by being radically redefined as argued by same-sex activists.

The argument that the marriage act should not be radically redefined is based on the fact that gays and lesbians already enjoy all the rights and privileges of de-facto couples. Long gone are the days when gays and lesbians were ostracised or discriminated against.

There's no doubt we are living in a time of significant social change, a time when social institutions such as marriage that have stood the test of time are being critiqued and undermined.

While some argue the benefits of such change, including increased autonomy, freedom and diversity, there is also an obvious downside. The English poet T. S. Eliot argues, 'by far the most important channel of transmission of culture remains the family: and when family fails to play its part, we must expect our culture to deteriorate'.

While not being as strident as Eliot it is true that family is central to a society's continued prosperity and growth. And central to the concept of family is the traditional definition of marriage.

The real agenda is for schools

The Catholic Weekly
20 September 2017

Advocates of same-sex marriage, including senior members of the Turnbull Government Simon Birmingham and Christopher Pyne, argue that a 'yes' vote will not adversely impact on religious freedom and the right to follow the church's teachings.

Supporters of same-sex marriage also argue the issue is simply about marriage equality and not about promoting a radical, cultural-left gender and sexuality agenda. Wrong on both accounts

Evidence from both here and overseas proves that if marriage is redefined to allow same-sex couples to marry then faith-based organisations, bodies and individuals will be penalised and made to suffer because of their religious beliefs and convictions.

In Victoria the owners of a holiday camp who refused to accommodate a gay/lesbian group were taken to court and financially penalised. In Tasmania an LGBTQI activist Martine Delaney lodged a complaint with the Anti-Discrimination Commissioner over the Catholic Church circulating its 'Don't mess with marriage' booklet to schools.

Given that both the Australian Labor Party and the Greens Party are committed to removing existing exemptions and exceptions to anti-discrimination laws relating to the ability to discriminate based on religious grounds then it's obvious that religious freedom will be under even greater threat if the definition of marriage is changed.

Overseas examples include a British Christian school having its performance downgraded as the Ofsted inspectors concluded it was 'homophobic' as it failed to teach the officially endorsed, secular view of LGBTQI diversity and difference.

In London a Jewish school enrolling girls aged three to eight was threatened with closure for not teaching the government's endorsed beliefs about gender fluidity and gender reassignment.

In America, under the Obama administration, schools were forced to allow transgender boys to use girls' toilets and changing rooms.

If the same-sex legislation is passed the reality is that schools in Australia will also be forced to implement a radical LGBTQI sexuality and gender agenda. The Australian Education Union, one of the most powerful teacher unions in Australia, in addition to supporting same sex marriage argues that 'Homosexuality and bisexuality need to be normalised' in the school curriculum and that 'All staff must be in-serviced in homophobia and hetero-sexism'.

The AEU policy for schools also argues it is wrong to believe that heterosexual relationships are 'natural' or 'normal' and condemns churches as 'un-Christian' for not accepting its cultural-left LGBTQI agenda.

It is also the case that the cultural-left has long sought to undermine Christianity and to banish religion from the public square and that the same-sex issue is part of a much broader campaign.

As argued by Aubrey Perry in a recent comment piece published in the Fairfax Press titled 'This survey is about much more than same sex marriage' the intention is to enforce a secular view of society, one where religion plays no part.

In relation to the SSM postal survey Perry argues: 'This survey offers us a conscious opportunity to make a firm stand in support of a secular government and to reject discrimination or favouritism based on religion. It's our opportunity to say that religion has no part in the shaping of our laws'.

ALP senator Penny Wong, in her Frank Walker Memorial Lecture, also suggests that there is no place for religion in law making when she argues 'The separation of church and state is one of the central planks on which liberal democracy stands'.

In relation to issues like same-sex marriage Wong argues: 'The problem in all of this, of course, is the application of religious belief to the framing of law in a secular society'.

If religion has no place one wonders why parliaments begin with the Lord's Prayer and why the Constitution includes the words, 'Humbly relying on the blessing of Almighty God'.

Roz Ward, the La Trobe University researcher responsible for the radical LGBTQI Safe Schools program that tells children gender is fluid and limitless, goes one step further and argues there is no place for a religious view of marriage as 'only Marxism provides the theory and practice of genuine human liberation'.

Ward goes on to argue 'Marxism offers both the hope and the strategy needed to create a world where human sexuality, gender and how we relate to our bodies can blossom in extraordinary new and amazing ways that we can only try to imagine today'.

Underpinning the campaign to change the definition of marriage is a radical LGBTQI gender ideology, described by Pope Francis as one 'which denies the difference and reciprocity in nature of a man and a woman and that envisages a society without gender differences, thereby removing the anthropological foundation of the family'.

The Pope also argues that defining marriage as involving people of the same sex 'leads to educational programmes and legislative guidelines which promote a personal identity and emotional intimacy radically separated from the biological difference between male and female'.

Our religious freedom is at society's heart

The Herald Sun
21 February 2018

There's no doubt that the Religious Freedom Review, commissioned by Prime Minister Turnbull in the context of last year's same-sex marriage debate and due to report by 31 March, is dealing with an issue central to our society and way of life.

And, as argued by Sydney's Archbishop Fisher, there's also no doubt that in an increasingly secular society: 'There is now a more hard-edge determination to minimise the role of faith in everyday life and exclude it altogether from the public square. Examples abound of this lack of tolerance for a religious worldview during the recent marriage debate'.

Along with freedom of speech, freedom of assembly, equality before the law, the right to vote and to live free of unjustified government interference the right to one's religious beliefs is what distinguishes our way of life to that experienced under totalitarian and oppressive regimes.

One of the key strategies used by communist and fascist dictatorships when exerting domination and control is to impose a secular, materialistic view of society — one where religion is banned and there is no higher authority than whoever controls the party and rules the state.

Such is the importance of religious freedom that international and local agreements guarantee it as a fundamental human right. The United Nation's 'Universal Declaration of Human Rights' states: 'Everyone has the right to freedom of thought, conscience and religion (and) to manifest his religion or belief in teaching, practice, worship and observance'.

The Victorian Charter also guarantees religious freedom when it argues: 'Every person has the right to freedom of thought, conscience, religion and belief, including: the freedom to demonstrate his or her religion or belief in worship, observance, practice and teaching'.

The Charter, legislated in 2006, also states 'A person must not be coerced or restrained in a way that limits his or her freedom to have or adopt a religion or belief in worship, observance, practice or teaching'.

Notwithstanding such guarantees it's obvious that religious freedom is under attack. At the extreme end are those who argue that there is no place for religion, especially Christianity, in Western societies like Australia.

The British atheist Richard Dawkins in *The God Delusion* argues there is no rational basis for religion or a belief in God and the afterlife. The Fairfax columnist Audrey Perry argues that Australians must 'reject discrimination or favouritism based on religion' and that 'religion has no part in shaping our laws'.

While not as extreme, another example relates to Archbishop Porteous being taken to Tasmania's anti-discrimination commission for circulating the Catholic Bishop's *Don't Mess With Marriage* booklet because it argued against same-sex marriage in the light of Church doctrine.

In Victoria a Christian Youth camp was fined for beaching the anti-discrimination laws because it refused to accept a booking from a gay/lesbian community health organisation.

Another example of religious intolerance involves those arguing that religious schools should not be able to discriminate in relation to employment — currently, schools are not forced to employ those who publicly contradict or are opposed to the religious nature and teachings of such schools.

The Greens Party's policy argues for 'the removal of religious exemptions from anti-discrimination laws' thus denying religious schools the right they currently have to decide who they employ.

In relation to employment the Australian Labor Party also poses as risk to Catholic schools and the Church's opposition to same-sex marriage by arguing that it will 'strengthen laws and expand programs against discrimination and harassment on the basis of sexual orientation, gender identity and intersex status'.

Overseas examples of religious freedom being threatened and curtailed abound and the danger, given the prevailing climate of political correctness and cultural-left, secular ideology, is that Australia will go down the same path.

Under President Obama American schools were forced to allow transgender students (boys who identified as girls or girls who identified as boys) to use the toilets of the gender they self-identified as.

In Canada a parent has been taken to court for wanting to withdraw his child from a radical gender and sexuality school program like Safe Schools that Premier Andrews is making compulsory for all Victorian government schools.

And in England both Jewish and Christian schools have been criticised and threatened with penalties by the education department's school inspectors for not teaching the government mandated cultural-left views about gender and sexuality

Religious freedom is an inherent right that distinguishes Western, liberal democracies from totalitarian regimes and is essential for the continued stability, social cohesion and peace of Australian society.

As such, it deserves to be protected against a secular agenda that seeks to banish religion from the public square and to deny the right religious bodies and individuals have to remain true to their faith.

The price of not mentioning the truth

The Catholic Weekly
15 April 2018

Archbishop Fisher's Easter warning that 'Powerful interests now seek to marginalise religious believers and beliefs, especially Christian ones, and exclude them from public life' is timely given the ever-increasing secular threat undermining Christian institutions and values.

During last year's debate about same-sex marriage Tasmania's Archbishop Porteous was threatened with being taken before the anti-discrimination commission for distributing the 'Don't Mess With Marriage' booklet to Catholic schools.

And those arguing in support of the traditional definition of marriage, instead of their arguments being evaluated objectively and impartially, were condemned as homophobic, heteronormative, transphobic and, worst of all, for being Christian.

Just witness the attacks on Australia's tennis great Margaret Court and rugby's Israel Folau for daring to question same-sex marriage and for suggesting that homosexuality runs counter to the Bible's teachings.

Other examples of ad hominem attacks include ex-prime minister Tony Abbott being vilified as the Mad Monk and the commonwealth member of parliament Kevin Andrews being condemned for introducing anti-euthanasia laws on the basis that he acted in the light of his Christian beliefs and values.

More recently a number of submissions to the Commonwealth inquiry into freedom of religion and beliefs also display an intense dislike for Christianity by seeking to remove current exceptions and exemptions to anti-discrimination laws.

Liberty Victoria's submission argues that freedom of religion should not be given special status on the basis, supposedly, that 'religious bodies have a long history of discriminating against and persecuting others' and that 'religious practices and behaviour cannot be above the law'.

The submission also argues that 'government policy and laws should not be based on religious beliefs' and that 'Religious practice that affects others, directly or indirectly, should have no special status'.

Not surprisingly, the submission from the Secular Party of Australia also argues that freedom of religion must be curtailed on the basis 'religion is a private, individual matter and religion should not impact the public square'.

Bizarrely, after equating Christianity with the more extremes of Islamic fundamentalism practised in Indonesia, Saudi Arabia and by Jihadist terrorists, the Secular Party also argues that governments must be secular because all forms of religion lead to violence and death.

Recommendations to the Commonwealth inquiry include banning government funding to religious schools, removing current exemptions granted to doctors and health professionals in relation to abortion and removing the freedom faith-based schools have over employment.

Even though existing state and territory legislation allows government schools to include formal Religious Instruction classes and teaching about religion in the general curriculum the submission from the Fairness In Religions In Schools seeks to banish religion from state schools.

Based on recent events in Quebec, the submission argues that parents' rights under international agreements to ensure their children's education accords with their personal religious convictions should no longer apply.

Instead Religious Instruction should be banned from government schools and education ministers should endorse a secular course in philosophy that eschews teaching about religious beliefs and values.

While a number of submissions to the Commonwealth inquiry argue religious bodies and individuals must be protected and religion is a vital element in public debate and policy it's clear that there are forces mobilising to enforce a secular, anti-Christian agenda.

In Victoria the socialist-left Andrews government has banned Religious Instruction classes from the formal school curriculum while mandating the Marxist-inspired Safe Schools gender and sexuality program for government schools.

A program that teaches students, even though approximately 98% of Australians identify as women and men, that gender is fluid and limitless and that boys can be girls and girls can be boys.

In Australia's national curriculum while students are told again and again across a range of subjects that they must learn to value and appreciate Aboriginal culture, history and spiritual beliefs Christianity's central role in Western civilisation and Australia's development as a nation is rarely, if ever, mentioned.

Ignored, as argued by Perth Based academic Augusto Zimmermann, is that Christianity underpins the Westminster form of government and the common law system we inherited from Britain that guarantees the freedoms and liberties we take for granted.

Also ignored, as argued by T. S. Eliot in *Notes Towards a Definition of Culture*, is that religion is vital to any culture and in relation to Western civilisations like Australia Christianity is central to what it is that makes as unique.

The 19th century aphorism 'eternal vigilance is the price of liberty' remains as true today as when it was first written and nowhere is this as important as when it relates to religious freedom.

As stated by Archbishop Fisher 'We cannot take the freedom to hold and practice our beliefs for granted, even here is Australia' and it is vital that committed Christians enter the public debate and win the battle of ideas.

Christ's soldiers need to heed the call to arms and champion their faith

The Australian
17 July 2018

While there is no doubt that religious freedom must be protected, it's equally true that Christians must be more assertive in entering the public square to champion what former British prime minister David Cameron termed a 'more muscular defence of our Judeo-Christian heritage'.

Given the rise of Islamic fundamentalism and the dangers of cultural relativism promoted by multiculturalism, Cameron argued that Christians must have 'the confidence to say 'yes', we are a Christian country and be proud of it'.

The argument that there is no place for Christianity as we are a secular society is only half true. The separation between church and state, unlike Islamic theocracies where religious doctrine is all-powerful, cannot disguise the reality that Western liberal democracies such as Australia are inherently Christian.

While epochal events such as the Enlightenment and the Reformation are significant and lasting in their impact, equally, if not more influential, is Western civilisation's Judeo-Christian heritage and ongoing beliefs and traditions.

It's no accident that parliaments around Australia, with the exception of the ACT, which is more like a local government authority, begin with the Lord's Prayer and that the preamble to the Constitution contains the words: 'Humbly relying on the blessing of almighty God.'

And while it is true that the percentage of Australians identifying as Christian has fallen to 52 per cent, according to the 2016 census, it is still the most dominant religion, with Islam at 2.6 per cent, Buddhism at 2.5 per cent and Hinduism 1.9 per cent.

Australia's legal and political systems can be understood only in the context of the New Testament and the teachings of Christ. As argued by Larry Siedentop in *Inventing the Individual* when tracing the historical development of Western civilisation, concepts such as the inherent dignity of the person and inalienable rights are deeply imbued with Christian morality.

Beginning with the impact of Christ's teachings in Rome and following a gradual evolution across hundreds of years in what is now Europe, Siedentop argues that the liberties and freedoms we take for granted at our peril are steeped in the word of God and the teachings of the church.

He writes that Christian beliefs 'lay the foundation for a new conception of society' based on individual conscience, free will and the need to love thy neighbour as thyself; a view of society where: 'There is neither Jew nor Greek, there is neither bond nor free, there is neither male nor female: for ye are all one in Christ Jesus.'

Perth-based academic Augusto Zimmermann, in a recent monograph titled *Christian Foundations of the Common Law*, also argues that our legal and political systems are indebted to Christianity.

When detailing the evolution of our common law system, Zimmermann writes: 'Indeed, there is little doubt that Christian philosophy influenced the origins and development of the English law.'

Zimmermann argues in relation to those living under English common law: 'This religious identity resulted in an enviable political environment whereby citizens could take their rights seriously, such as by considering these rights to be God-given and not government acquired.'

Not surprisingly, the American Freedom House ranks those countries associated with Christianity, including the US, Australia, New Zealand, Canada and Britain, highest in terms of democratic rights, including freedom of religion, speech, assembly and the press. Countries to our north, including China, Myanmar, Cambodia, Vietnam and Laos, as well as those under the yoke of communist dictatorships and Islamic fundamentalism, are ranked at the bottom of the freedom index.

Such is the freedom and liberty we take for granted that millions of migrants and refugees are flooding into Europe — and, if not for the Howard government policy of border protection, also would be arriving on our shores.

And while there's no doubt that Christianity has been guilty of many transgressions, ranging from religious persecution to the evil crime of paedophilia, it is also true that its saving grace is the ability and willingness to acknowledge the sins of the past, to reform and better contribute to the common good.

As argued in a values statement signed by 22 Christian leaders and presented to the British House of Commons, Christianity is responsible for 'the struggles to establish the rule of law and to defeat slavery and the slave trade; the establishment of the rights of conscience and the consistent opposition to intimidation, coercion, corruption, tyranny and oppression; the founding of numerous charitable institutions and the upholding of human dignity'.

As detailed in *The Black Book of Communism*, totalitarian dictators such as Stalin, Mao, Pol Pot and Kim Il-sung, on the other hand, are guilty of starving, murdering and executing about 94 million people in the forlorn and impossible hope of establishing a socialist utopia.

As Islamic terrorism is on the rise and secular nihilism is increasingly pervasive, the irony, Douglas Murray points out in *The Strange Death of Europe*, is that Christianity is ignored and undermined.

Given the existential threat confronting Western civilisation, Murray also makes the point that unless those in the West rediscover and champion what makes their culture so unique and worth preserving, they are destined to be foreigners in their own land.

The real goal is banning Faith

The Catholic Weekly
18 October 2018

Make no mistake, the debate surrounding whether religious schools should have the right to decide who they enrol and who they employ is simply the most recent illustration of the cultural-left's campaign to destroy religious freedom, banish Christianity from public life and to radically change society.

And one of the most powerful and successful strategies used by the cultural-left seeking to remake society in its Marxist image is to embark on the long march where, instead of a revolution, change occurs incrementally and the final destination is hidden.

The cultural-left's gender and sexuality Safe Schools campaign provides a striking example. While marketed as an attempt to respect gender diversity and difference and to stop bullying the real rationale, as admitted by one of its designers, is to indoctrinate students with a Marxist inspired view of gender.

Roz Ward argues 'only Marxism provides the theory and practice of genuine human liberation' and the 'Safe Schools Coalition is about supporting gender and sexual diversity, not about stopping bullying'.

Changing the marriage act last year to include gays and lesbians provides another example. As admitted by Aubrey Perry in a comment piece published in the Fairfax Press the same-sex marriage campaign was simply the first step in removing religion from our way of life.

Perry revealed this Marxist inspired secular agenda when she argued

'This survey offers us a conscious opportunity to make a firm stand in support of a secular government and to reject discrimination or favouritism based on religion. It's our opportunity to say that religion has no part in the shaping of our laws'.

Ignored, as argued by Augusto Zimmerman that Christianity underpins our political and legal systems and that parliaments around Australia begin with the Lord's Prayer.

One only needs to look at the responses to the leaked Ruddock Report's recommendations about religious freedom to realise the full significance of what the cultural-left is seeking to achieve.

Religious schools currently have the right to discriminate in terms of who they enrol and who they employ and that right is now threatened. Journalists and commentators at the ABC and in the Fairfax press are leading the campaign to deny schools the right to manage themselves according to their religious convictions.

And once religious schools lose the right to remain true to their faith, expect that the next step will be to force such schools to implement a radical gender and sexuality curriculum like the Marxist inspired Safe Schools program.

A program the Victorian government, while removing religious education from the school curriculum, has asked government schools to implement.

Central to such programs is the argument that even though 98 per cent of Australians are happy to be female or male there is nothing natural or normal in being heterosexual and that boys have the right to self-identify as girls and girls to self-identify as boys.

LGBTQI activists also argue that boys who self-identify as girls have the right to wear a girl's uniform, change in the girls' changing room and be involved in girls' sports. Based on events in the UK where religious schools are being penalised for not teaching the government mandated

LGBTQI curriculum, also expect faith based Australian schools to suffer.

A second strategy employed by those seeking to destroy religion, especially Christianity, is to couch the debate in terms of whether faith-based schools, hospitals, age care homes and other facilities should be exempted from anti-discrimination laws.

Instead of treating religious freedom as an inherent right that must be protected, like freedom of speech and freedom of conscience, it is treated as secondary to other rights like the right to be a LGBTQI person and be employed in a religious school.

As argued by associate professor Neil Foster from the University of Newcastle, instead of being considered an inherent right in Australia 'religious freedom is buried in clauses to discrimination acts and is not given proper recognition as a fundamental human right'. Unlike overseas where the 'International Covenant on Civil and Political Rights' endorses the right faith-based schools have to act according to their religious beliefs when it argues parents have the right 'to ensure the religious and moral education of their children (is) in conformity with their own convictions'.

The 'Convention Against Discrimination in Education' also argues that governments must protect the freedom parents have 'to ensure that religious and moral education of the children is in conformity with their own convictions'. To force faith-based schools to act against the religious convictions of parents enrolling their children is to deny an inherent human right.

As argued by Cardinal George Pell 'Christians believe that everyone should be free from unjust discrimination, but anti-discrimination laws which do not respect fundamental human rights, such as freedom of religion and conscience, are unjust laws'.

Ignorance and Islamism are our greatest threats

The Australian
20 November 2018

Civilisations rise and fall and, as T. S. Eliot argues in *Notes Towards a Definition of Culture*, once a civilisation turns its back on its cultural heritage and enemies threaten its way of life, it is in danger of ceasing to exist.

Based on events here and overseas, it's clear that Western civilisation is under threat as a result of being attacked by Islamic terrorism while being undermined by an education system that fails to acknowledge and defend the strengths and benefits of our culture and way of life.

English academic Roger Scruton, in his book *Culture Counts: Faith and Feeling in a World Besieged*, says Western societies 'are experiencing an acute crisis of identity' as a result of an external threat represented by radical Islam and the impact of cultural relativism and multiculturalism from within.

Douglas Murray puts a similar argument in *The Strange Death of Europe* when he says 'Europe has lost faith in its beliefs, traditions and legitimacy', caused by a failure to assert the primacy of Western civilisation by those normally expected to celebrate and defend it and the destructive impact of mass migration of mainly young Muslim men and the rise of Islamic fundamentalism.

Australia also is facing a crisis in the legitimacy of Western civilisation caused by a non-discriminatory migration policy leading to ethnic enclaves and the threat of Islamic terrorism as well as a loss of faith in our cultural heritage, institutions and way of life as a result of cultural relativism and the impact of cultural-left theory.

The hostile reaction by academics at the Australian National University and the University of Sydney to the establishment of a centre dedicated to teaching Western civilisation illustrates how the cultural Left now controls the academy.

A total of 150 academics and staff at the University of Sydney signed an open letter that states: 'The Ramsay program represents, quite simply, European supremacism writ large: it signals that the study of the European cultural tradition warrants better educational circumstances than that of others.'

The argument that there is nothing superior or more beneficial about Western civilisation, thus placing it on the same footing as Aboriginal and Torres Strait Islander, Eskimo and New Guinea tribal cultures, ignores the reality that one is more civilised.

Forget the misplaced romantic ideal of the noble savage associated with 18th-century French philosopher Jean-Jacques Rousseau; the reality is that life among less civilised tribes was often nasty, brutish and short.

At the same time, cultural-left academics mistakenly argued that all cultures were equal as they also embarked on the long march through the education system to radically reshape how subjects such as history, literature, art, music and politics were taught.

As British conservative politician Michael Gove says in *Celsius 7/7*, old-style Marxism, with its economic focus on overthrowing capitalism, has long since morphed into a rainbow —alliance of theories, including neo-Marxism, postmodernism, deconstruction and feminist, gender, queer and postcolonial theories.

While such theories vary in their focus and are often in disagreement, they are all involved in the culture wars and are deeply committed to radically reshaping the institutions, beliefs, values and cultural heritage associated with Western civilisation.

The Australian national curriculum provides ample evidence of how successful the cultural Left is in indoctrinating students. We are described as a 'multicultural, secular and multi-faith society' where diversity and difference reign supreme and there is no recognition that Judeo-Christianity has played, and continues to play, a prominent role.

While there are hundreds of references to Aboriginal and Torres Strait Islander history, culture and spirituality, there is no detailed and substantial treatment of the grand narrative associated with the evolution of Western civilisation and epochal events such as the Enlightenment and the Age of Reason.

And compared with students being taught about the flaws and weaknesses associated with Western civilisation (slavery, environmental destruction, inequality and discrimination) they are told that Indigenous cultures are 'strong, resilient, rich and diverse', with no mention of alcohol and drug abuse, sexual exploitation and violence against girls and women.

At a time when it has never been more important to safeguard against Islamic terrorism and there is a need to promote a commitment to and love of one's country, the national curriculum also champions a decidedly cultural-left, subjective interpretation of citizenship.

Teachers are told: 'Citizenship means different things to people at different times and, depending on personal perspectives, their social situation and where they live. This is reflected in multiple perspectives of citizenship that reflect personal, social, spatial and temporal dimensions of citizenship.'

If there is no agreed, common meaning of what citizenship entails, then there is nothing wrong with Islamic fundamentalists with Australian citizenship travelling overseas to join the jihad against the West, then returning to Australia radicalised by the experience.

What's to be done? Former British prime minister David Cameron says the first thing to do is to champion what he describes as muscular liberalism. Western civilisation has given the world a robust, democratic system of government based on liberty and freedom that must be defended. He also says, as did Tony Abbott as prime minister, that those who wish to live in the West regardless of their culture, religion or political beliefs must abide by the laws of their new land and not import foreign hostilities and grievances.

Education also needs to play a major role in addressing the threat posed by enemies foreign and domestic. Without being xenophobic, racist or unfairly discriminatory, it is vital that students in schools and universities are introduced to and become familiar with the grand narrative associated with Western civilisation — a civilisation, notwithstanding its faults and sins, that is responsible for the kind of peace, stability and high standard of living unprecedented in the history of mankind and that is the envy of billions across the globe.

As argued by Pierre Ryckmans in his 1996 Boyer lectures, it is also impossible for Australian students to understand foreign cultures such as China unless they have a detailed and comprehensive understanding of their own.

Secularism — the new firebrand religion

Spectator Australia
16 February 2019

The Australian Senate is currently considering a bill sponsored by the ALP's Senator Wong, if accepted, that will amend the *Sex Discrimination Act 1984* to remove 'the capacity of bodies established for religious purposes that provide education to directly discriminate against students on the basis of their sexual orientation, gender identity or intersex status'.

The Senate inquiry, due to report by the 11 February, should be seen in the context of last year's Ruddock review of religious freedom that investigated how best to protect the inherent right we all have to follow the religion of our choice and the right religious bodies have to act according to their faith.

Also important is that ALP and the Greens Party policies are directed at ending the right religious organisations currently have over who the employ and how they manage themselves.

That the ALP intends to compromise religious freedom is proven by the resolution carried at the recent national conference stating the party 'will act against all forms of discrimination and harmonise antidiscrimination laws and procedures' across Australia.

In particular, the ALP's resolution refers to the elimination of discrimination on the grounds of 'class, race, sex, sexual orientation, gender identity, intersex status, religion, political affiliation, national origin, citizenship, ages, disability, regional location, economic or household status'.

In relation to faith-based schools the Greens Party also argues that the current exemptions granted to religious organisations should be repealed and that education bodies no longer be allowed to discriminate 'on the basis of sex, sexual orientation, lawful sexual activity, marital status, parental status or gender identity'.

Even the Australian Education Union, instead of focusing on rectifying students' poor literacy and numeracy results, argues the right currently held by faith-based schools over enrolments and staffing must be abolished. It should also be noted that there is no evidence that faith-based schools have ever acted against an LGBTQI student.

The AEU's acting president Meredith Pearce believes that religious schools should not have the right to discriminate in relation to who they enrol or who they employ on the basis that 'No school should have the right to turn away or discriminate against LGBTIQ students or teachers'.

It's also clear that the left-of-centre parties want to force faith-based schools to implement radical gender and sexuality programs like Safe Schools — programs that tell young boys they can self-identify as girls and that that there is nothing unique or special about the love between a woman and a man for the purpose of procreation.

Taken to its logical conclusion forcing religious schools to deny critical aspects of their faith has far wider implications. The intention is that the school curriculum will impose a secular view of gender and sexuality and transgender students will be allowed to use the toilets and changing rooms of those students they self-identify as.

As with what is currently happening under a Western Australian ALP government, where Marxist inspired gender and sexuality programs are being forced on schools, expect the same to happen nationally if Bill Shorten becomes Prime Minister.

One only needs to note recent events in the United Kingdom where, in order to force schools to teach so-called 'British values' faith-based schools have been pressured by Ofsted to implement a radical, secular approach to gender and sexuality to see what will soon be happening in Australia.

A private Jewish school, the Vishnitz Girls School, has been evaluated as a failed school three times by Ofsted inspectors for not teaching girls under the age of eight about gender reassignment and sexuality. According to Jibran Khan, a Fellow at the National Review Institute, six other faith-based schools were also targeted and penalised.

Khan also makes the point that the agenda behind the campaign to restrict the religious freedom enjoyed by faith-based schools is part of a broader secular humanist attack on religion described as 'coercive secularism'. The British Chief Inspector of Education is quoted as arguing the State has the right to 'use compulsory education to make sure children acquire a deep understanding and respect for the British values'. Even if such values contradict the religious beliefs of parents and schools.

Debates about the Ruddock review and events in Western Australia and Victoria illustrate a much larger battle between secular critics and those committed to Judeo-Christianity and the importance of religious inspiration and faith to the nation's history and well-being.

Proven by last year's debate about same-sex marriage there are those who argue religious beliefs must be ignored. In the Fairfax Press Aubrey Perry argued 'This survey offers us a conscious opportunity to make a firm stand in support of a secular government and to reject discrimination or favouritism based on religion. It's our opportunity to say that religion has no part in the shaping of our laws'.

The irony is that while secular critics criticise and undermine Judeo-Christianity and its teachings about the spiritual and transcendent sense of life and death they celebrate and applaud Aboriginal and Torres Strait Islander spiritual beliefs and religious traditions.

In the national curriculum in subjects like history, literature, music, art and civics Christianity is rarely if ever mentioned and there is no recognition of the central importance of the New Testament's commitment to the inherent dignity of the person and the right each individual has to liberty and freedom.

Indigenous culture and religion, on the other hand, receive hundreds of references in almost every subject from kindergarten to Year 10. And the portrayal, much like Rousseau's idea of the noble savage, is always positive with no recognition that there might be any shortcomings or flaws.

The reality is secularism, which has become the new religion of the 21st century, has no right to consider itself preeminent and no right to deny religious freedom to those individuals and faith based institutions that seek to remain true to their conscience and faith. To do otherwise is to compromise a fundamental human right essential to liberty and that Western, liberal democracies like Australia must continue to protect.

When the centre does not hold

The Catholic Weekly
5 April 2019

Gone are the times when marriage was solely a sacrament involving a woman and a man for the purpose of procreation, people dressed discreetly and modestly, TV shows like *Married at First Sight* were unheard of and children knew nothing about sexting or internet pornography.

We know live in a world saturated with radical gender and sexuality theory and what the Italian intellectual Augusto Del Noce describes as 'eroticism'. Evidence includes sexually suggestive TV advertisements and sitcoms, pornography rampant on the internet, the Sydney Gay and Lesbian Mardi Gras and Marxist inspired gender bending programs like Safe Schools.

A program that tells primary school children there is nothing normal or beneficial about marriage involving a woman and a man, that they can decide for themselves whether they are lesbian, gay, queer or in transition and that society is heteronormative, transphobic and misogynist.

One only has to look at Tasmania where the parliament is considering a bill to stop recording a baby's gender at birth, to allow anyone over 16 to change their gender by simply signing a statutory declaration and where fines will be introduced to penalise 'misgendering' to realise how society has changed.

When detailing the rise of eroticism and sexual promiscuity across the Western world Del Noce refers to Wilhelm Reich's iconic book *The Sexual Revolution*. Although published in 1930 Del Noce makes the point that

Reich's book was rediscovered during the 1960s cultural revolution and that it had and continues to have a profound effect.

The late '60s was a time of dramatic change and upheaval represented by Vietnam moratoriums and demonstrations, sexual liberation and the 'pill', a revolt against established authority including the church and the rise of identity politics and victimhood.

As noted by the Australian academic Michael Liccione the late '60s 'was one of the most significant years of the 20th century, at least in the Western world'. The then Cardinal Ratzinger makes a similar point when suggesting the 1960s cultural revolution, in particular, has had a profound impact on Christianity.

Ratzinger writes the '60s generation of cultural-left intellects and activists 'conceived the whole evolution of history, beginning with the triumph of Christianity, as an error and a failure'. As well as adversely affecting the Church's teachings regarding marriage and sexuality Ratzinger also notes the rise or relativism and the denial of objectivity and truth as a result of postmodern theory.

Today's world, according to Ratzinger, is one where 'we are building a dictatorship of relativism that does not recognise anything as definitive and whose ultimate goal consists solely of one's own ego and desires'.

As a result, schools and universities now teach that wisdom, spirituality and truth are social constructs enforcing the power and hegemony of the capitalist ruling class and that the Bible is merely one text among many that has to be critiqued and deconstructed in terms of the new trinity of gender, ethnicity and class.

University academics across Australia are also eager to argue that the history of Western civilisation, especially Christianity, is one of violence, oppression, intimidation and colonial exploitation and that those who defend Western culture are guilty of advocating 'white supremacy' and 'European essentialism'.

The consequences of the '60s cultural revolution and the type of sexual liberation advocated by Wilhelm Reich are clear to see. As noted by Liccione 'What once seemed like divine commands securely rooted in human nature are now seen as irrational and arbitrary prejudices'.

Best illustrated by the slogan 'love is love' championed during the same-sex marriage debate we know live in a society where there are no absolutes or moral truths guiding how we perceive ourselves and how we interact with others.

Instead of serving the common good and seeking what Aristotle describes as the good life founded on virtues such as temperance, justice, prudence and courage happiness and fulfilment are now defined in terms of ego and self-gratification.

Whereas only a short time ago society considered abortion as a medical procedure of last resort, state sanctioned killing was abhorred, having children outside marriage was shunned and gender was binary we are now in a world, to quote W. B. Yeats, where 'The Best lack all conviction, while the worst are full of passionate intensity'.

While there is no doubt that Christianity, especially Catholicism, is suffering as a result of the evil and unforgiveable crime of child abuse it is vital to acknowledge that without spirituality and faith society will only continue to deteriorate and people's lives will remain empty and bereft of joy and hope.

The reality is that to be human is to yearn for a deeper and more lasting sense of meaning and transcendence than what is offered by today's materialistic, self-centred culture where secular critics argue God is dead and religion is the opiate of the masses.

Easter: the search for meaning

The Catholic Weekly
18 April 2019

What does Easter mean for you? For many, in an increasingly materialistic and pleasure driven society it's all about hot cross buns, chocolate Easter eggs and an extended weekend with family and friends.

For Christians, on the other hand, Easter involves the betrayal, death and resurrection of Christ and the knowledge that while this world might be a vale of tears if one embraces the word of God there will be eternal deliverance and salvation.

Easter is a time of contemplation, spiritual renewal and reaffirming the belief that all is not lost no matter how difficult and painful life is. In suffering and pain there is the possibility of redemption and in death there is rebirth.

Notwithstanding its religious significance there is no denying that Easter is now very much a secular occasion and there is less and less recognition that for Christians it is one of the most significant and holy events of the liturgical year.

For many adults the most important thing about Easter is time off work and for many children it is the expectation of finding the most chocolate Easter eggs hidden around the house and garden.

Increasingly, our society, as detailed by the Italian philosopher and academic Augusto Del Noce in *The Crisis of Modernity*, is one where religion no longer resonates in people's lives as it once did and where the parables and moral lessons of the New Testament are largely forgotten or ignored.

Fewer and fewer Australians now understand what the Good Samaritan refers to, the significance of the parable of the lost son or why it is important to turn the other cheek. Worse still many young people lack a strong moral and ethical compass and fail to distinguish between good and evil.

Undermining religion is the rise of a hedonistic society where instant gratification and sensual pleasures dominate our way of life. Voyeuristic shows like *Marriage at First Sight* celebrate narcissism, betrayal and relationships based on self-interest and a lack of long-term commitment and willingness to compromise.

Religion has also been weakened by science and the belief that the only things that are true are those that can be physically proven; the Marxist belief that religion is the opiate of the masses and a postmodern philosophy that argues there are no absolutes as everything is subjective and relative.

For years now in our schools and universities students have been taught that there is nothing inherently beneficial or worthwhile about knowledge or education for its own sake. Based on the rise of neo-Marxist critical theory the argument is that knowledge is a social construct employed by the elites to dominate and control the marginalised and dispossessed.

Add the evil stain of child abuse and it's understandable why when Christianity is mentioned so many express hatred and disgust. Given religion has been banished from the school curriculum it's also understandable why so many are ignorant about why Christianity and why the Bible is such a vital part of Western civilisation and our daily lives.

Few know that parliaments around Australia begin with the Lord's Prayer and that the preamble to the Australian Constitution contains the words 'Humbly relying on the blessing of Almighty God'. Even fewer realise that concepts like free will, the inherent dignity of the person and the importance of having a conscience are derived from the New Testament.

While secular critics celebrate that we are now living in a post-Christian age Easter is also a time to evaluate what has been lost as a result of embracing this brave new world controlled by technocrats, sceptics and those championing politically correct victimhood and identity politics.

Based on the appalling statistics around drug abuse, self-harm, depression and suicide it is obvious young people, in particular, need more than just digital technology and social networking sites to be resilient and to be able to cope with life's challenges and threats.

What spirituality and transcendence offers is a sense that one is not alone and that there is a higher and more lasting sense of meaning and fulfilment that can assuage the suffering and loss that is an inevitable part of what it means to be human.

At a time of widespread uncertainty and doubt, what the poet W. B. Yeats describes as a period where 'The best lack all conviction, while the worst are full of passionate intensity' it is also true that religion provides a compelling moral and spiritual framework in which to evaluate others and to act.

Illustrated by the reaction to the appalling and distressing destruction of Notre Dame, where groups of Parisians wept and sang hymns, religion also provides a sense of community, kinship and bonding that is much needed in what is an increasingly fragmented and solitary world.

Persecution of Christians taken to extreme

The Australian
24 April 2019

The barbaric and evil attack on Christians in Sri Lanka is yet a further illustration of what Christian activist Patrick Sookhdeo in *The Death of Western Christianity* describes as Christianophobia: 'a state of fear and hatred against Christianity and Christians'.

Sookhdeo argues that we are living across the globe in an intolerant and oppressive 'anti-Christian age' where those committed to the Bible suffer oppression and violence, and in extreme cases torture and death.

In China the communist government creates a climate of fear and intimidation where Christians are treated as second-class citizens and the Catholic Church is denied the freedom to act independently of government.

In Egypt the Christian Copts are also oppressed: in April 2017, on Palm Sunday, 45 worshippers were killed when two churches were bombed by Islamist terrorists. A year earlier in Pakistan, 75 Christians were killed and hundreds injured while celebrating Easter in an attack by Islamist militants.

And as explained in the just-released book *The Thirty-Year Genocide* by Benny Morris and Dror Ze'evi, detailing the treatment of Christians in what is now Turkey, there is a long history in the Middle East of extreme and inhumane violence and cruelty.

During the period from 1894 to 1924, covering the last years of the Ottoman Empire and the establishment of the Turkish republic, Christians suffered under a state-mandated strategy of 'premeditated mass killing, homicidal deportation, forced conversion, mass rape and brutal abduction'. Indeed, such is the barbaric treatment currently inflicted on Christians that Muslim commentator and author Mehdi Hasan argues online in The Intercept that commentators and politicians in the West should do more to acknow ledge their brutal and merciless treatment.

After noting the widespread condemnation in response to the horrific attack on the mosques in Christchurch, Hasan writes: 'I am a Muslim, and I consider myself to be on the left, but I'm embarrassed to admit that in both Muslim and left circles the issue of Christian persecution has been downplayed and even ignored for far too long.'

As to why there is an aversion in the West to admitting Christians are suffering and that more needs to be done to make public what is happening, the reasons are many and complex.

Italian academic Augusto Del Noce, in *The Crisis of Modernity*, argues the prevailing orthodoxy dominating the West is one of secular humanism inspired by neo-Marxism, critical theory and scientific rationalism. Since the end of World War I, Christianity as a moral and spiritual system based on the New Testament and the word of God has been supplanted by an ideology committed to creating a man-made utopia based on empiricism and the belief that political and economic factors determine how societies are structured.

Such is the hostility that secular critics argue we are living in a post-Christian age where the belief system based on the New Testament that has nourished and underpinned Western civilisation for thousands of years is obsolete and irrelevant.

As detailed by Cardinal Joseph Ratzinger, later Pope Benedict XVI, the dominant mode of thinking and relating to others and the world at large is characterised by relativism and subjectivism. Christianity, on the other hand, is based on the word of God and the conviction that there are absolutes.

In this postmodern world of critical theory the Bible is simply one text among many that has to be critiqued and deconstructed in terms of power relationships and how it imposes a Eurocentric, mis ogynist and heteronormative view of the world — one guilty of privileging whiteness.

The subservience to multiculturalism and uncritically celebrating diversity and difference also help to explain why Christianity is not being given the recognition and attention it deserves.

For years schools and universities have taught students that there is nothing special or unique about Christianity and that all cultures and belief systems deserve the same recognition (with the exception of Western civilisation).

Best illustrated by the national curriculum, Christianity is absent or considered on the same footing as Indigenous spirituality. Harmony Day and Sorry Day are on the same level as Christmas and Easter, and Dreamtime stories are given the same emphasis as Genesis.

Evidenced by those hundreds of academics who have signed open letters condemning universities for entertaining the possibility of hosting a Ramsay Centre for Western Civilisation, the aversion to Christianity is widespread in the academy.

The hostility and indifference to Christianity in Australia is not limited to schools and universities. Whether it's the ABC's *The Drum* and *Q&A* or *The Age* and *The Sydney Morning Herald*, most commentators are cultural-left and more concerned about identity politics and politically correct victimhood than the plight of Christians.

Safeguard freedom of religion and freedom of speech in Australia

The Daily Telegraph
30 May 2019

There's no doubt that threats to religious freedom and freedom of expression are factors explaining Bill Shorten's defeat and the re-election of the Scott Morrison government. While the ALP's high taxation policies, failure to support the Adani coal mine and Shorten's unpopularity contributed to the loss concerns about such freedoms also impacted on the result.

Normally, the ALP can rely on working class electorates for support but not in this election. While the ALP won votes in wealthy, privileged electorates it lost votes in traditional Labor seats with large numbers of voters from conservative religious and ethnic backgrounds.

While not directly an election issue Israel Folau's appalling and unjustified treatment for quoting the Bible when arguing that unless they repented homosexuals and other sinners would suffer in hell highlighted religious freedom as an issue.

And given the high number of conservative religious and ethnic voters in western Sydney it should not surprise that Chris Bowen suffered a 5.4% swing against him in his seat of McMahon. These are the same electors that registered one of the highest 'no' votes against the same-sex marriage legislation proposed in 2016.

While there's no doubt that the Adani coal mine was a significant issue in Queensland it's also true that religion played a role in stopping the ALP winning any seats north of Brisbane. Many of the communities in these electorates are evangelical Christians anxious about the increasing threat posed by politically correct, cultural-left critics.

In Melbourne's Chisholm electorate, one that the ALP had counted on as a win, religion also had a strong influence as many of the voters in the large Chinese community saw the ALP's policies as undermining the traditional family by pushing a radical gender and sexuality agenda.

And based on the polices of the ALP and the Greens parties there's no doubt that those of religious faith had every reason to fear a possible Bill Shorten government. In the weeks before the election the shadow attorney-general Mark Dreyfus signalled that an ALP government would not appoint a religious freedom commissioner to the Human Rights Commission.

Instead Dreyfus stated there would be an LGBTIQ commissioner and that in line with the ALP's *A Fair Go For LGBTIQ* policy faith-based schools and other educational bodies would no longer have the freedom to appoint staff and enrol students who supported their religious teachings.

The policy statement, after admitting legislating same-sex marriage 'wasn't the end of the road', states that schools would no longer have the freedom to discriminate 'against students and staff on the basis of their sexuality or gender identity'.

Add the fact that Greens Party intended to legislate a Charter of Rights to 'remove religious exemptions in federal anti-discrimination laws' and to reintroduce the Marxist inspired Safe Schools gender and sexuality program and it's understandable why religious voters preferred a coalition government.

What the ALP failed to consider is that out of the nearly 3.9 million students across Australia Catholic schools enrol approximately 20 per cent and independent mainly faith-based schools over 14 per cent; the parents of such students wanted their schools to have the freedom to embody their religious beliefs.

Given Bill Shorten's failure to defend Israel Folau's right to express his religious convictions about homosexuality and Scott Morrison's willingness to allow Australians to see him worshipping in his Pentecostal Church it's understandable why the ALP failed to win.

While Shorten lacked credibility and authenticity Morrison successfully presented himself as genuine person with deeply held morals and beliefs that resonated with outer suburban and regional voters; what commentators described as the Howard Battlers and who Morrison rebadged as the silent Australians.

It's ironic that at the same time orthodox religion played a significant role in explaining the outcome of the election it's also true that the ALP's unquestioning commitment to the secular religion of climate change had an impact.

By worshiping Mother Earth and embracing a deep green view of global warming the ALP convinced voters that the cost of electricity and gas would continue to rise and that Australia's standard of living would continue to deteriorate.

Especially in the mining states of Queensland and Western Australia, far removed from the soy milk, free-trade latte inner city dwellers of Sydney and Melbourne, voters decided that work was better than virtue signalling and that coal was preferable to unreliable and expensive solar and wind power.

The challenge for the Morrison Government is now to deliver on its promise to safeguard freedom of religion and freedom of speech. Voters will await the outcome of the current review of religious freedom undertaken by the Law Reform Commission, in particular, to judge whether the new government is fair dinkum.

Fighting back in the gender wars

Spectator Australia
22 June 2019

Israel Folau is right to condemn gender fluidity and the push to get children and adolescents to transition. For far too long radical Marxist inspired programs like Safe Schools have been pushed on schools and children taught to believe that boys can be girls and girls can be boys — or any of the over 40 LGBTIQ+ categories in between.

And Folaus' intervention in the gender wars is timely given last week's release of the Catholic Church's *Male and Female He Created Them*.

The Church document warns about a 'crisis in education' where children are mistakenly taught gender is limitless and they can self-identify as whatever gender they desire. In opposition to radical gender theory the Church argues it is wrong to deny 'the biological differences between male and female'.

Gender is not a social construct as 99 per cent of babies are born with XX or XY chromosomes and this determines whether they are female or male. And it's not just the Folau and Church in Rome arguing it is wrong to deny the binary nature of gender and sexuality.

The American College of Pediatricians also argues 'human sexuality is an objective biological trait' that 'is binary by design with the obvious purpose being the reproduction and flourishing of our species'.

Instead of being an anti-bullying program one of Safe Schools designers Roz Ward argues it's designed to impose radical LGBTIQ+ theory on schools.

Ward admits the intention of the program is to 'create a world where human sexuality, gender and how we relate to our bodies can blossom in extraordinary new and amazing ways that we can only try to imagine today'.

One of the resources associated with Safe Schools argues 'sexuality can't really be defined' and that 'sexuality is fluid and changes over time'. Students are also told 'What you label yourself is up to you'.

In opposition to schools being told to indoctrinate students with radical gender ideology the Church document stresses the 'primary rights and duties of parents with regard to the education of their children'.

The Church's argument that parental responsibilities 'cannot be delegated or usurped by others' is supported by the 'International Covenant on Civil and Political Rights' that states governments must respect the liberty of parents 'to ensure the religious and moral education of their children (is) in conformity with their own convictions'.

At a time when religious freedom is threatened and where the Commonwealth Government is yet to decide its full response to the Ruddock Religious Freedom Review the Church also signals that Catholic schools need to remain true to their religious teachings and beliefs.

In relation to gender programs like Safe Schools the Church document argues governments should respect the 'legitimate aspirations of Catholic Schools to maintain their own vision of human sexuality'.

Such a warning is especially important given the experience of Christian and other faith-based schools in England penalised for failing to implement a secular, state mandated view of gender that contradicts their teachings.

By questioning radical gender theory the Church's document also serves as a timely warning about the impact of teaching students there is nothing wrong with changing their gender.

One of the outcomes of radical programs like Safe Schools has been the dramatic increase in children undergoing hormonal treatment and reassignment. In Sydney, for example, over the last 10 years there has been a dramatic increase in new patients seeking gender reassignment at major public hospitals.

The dangers associated with gender reassignment include the high rates of depression and self-harm experienced when adolescent children enter adulthood and realise too late that what they initially had been taught to believe was untrue.

Such are the dangers associated with gender transition (known as gender dysphoria) that the American College of Pedetricians recommends 'health professionals, educators and legislators to reject all policies that condition children to accept a life of chemical and surgical impersonation of the opposite sex as normal and healthful'.

And counter to those arguing those opposed to gender theory are conservative and out of touch it's significant that the American feminist Camille Paglia (who describes herself a 'non-gendered identity') also argues gender is binary.

In her book *Free Women Free Men* Paglia argues 'except in very rare conditions of true hermaphroditism the DNA of every cell of the human body is inflexibly coded as male or female from birth to death'.

Paglia also argues 'without knowledge of biology, gender studies slides into propaganda' and warns against what she describes as 'Extravaganzas of gender experimentation'.

There's no doubt that radical gender theory is impacting on what is taught in schools and society more broadly, even in sport where men who have transitioned now compete against women. At the same time the Catholic Church's document and Folau's opposition offer much needed counter arguments that need to be heard.

Truth is the first casualty of the gender wars

The Catholic Weekly
19 July 2019

The release of the Congregation for Catholic Education's publication *Male and Female He Created Them: Towards a path of dialogue on the question of gender theory in education* is timely and relevant; especially in Australia where radical gender and sexuality programs like Safe Schools are commonplace.

Such programs treat gender and sexuality as social constructs that are fluid and limitless and advise students they have the power to self-identify as any of a multiplicity of categories including: gay, lesbian, transgender, queer, intersex, non-binary and genderfluid.

The Vatican document is right to warn against the destructive influence of gender theory and to quote Genesis: 'male and female he created them'.

One of the first casualties of war is the truth and when it comes to the gender wars this is certainly the case. In their campaign to spread a radical, Marxist inspired view of gender and sexuality the LGBTIQ+ thought police are guilty of misinformation and basic errors of fact.

In the *All of Us* booklet distributed to schools as part of the Safe Schools program the claim is made '10 per cent of people are same sex attracted', '4 per cent of people are transgender or gender diverse' and '1.7 per cent of people are intersex' – a total of 15.7 per cent.

Inflating the figure not only gives the impression that a significant number of Australians are gender diverse and fluid, it also leads students to believe that identifying as LGBTIQ+ is a normal part of expressing one's gender and sexual identity.

Contrary to the argument that 15.7 per cent of Australians are LGBTIQ+ research proves the figure is closer to 3 to 5 per cent.

Based on three national surveys, researchers at Charles Darwin University conclude that what they describe as non-heterosexuals account for about 3.2 per cent of the population.

Non-heterosexuals are described as 'all those who identify as gay, homosexual, lesbian or bisexual, or construct their sexuality in other ways using non-heterosexual terminology (eg queer)'.

Academics from the University of Queensland in a paper published on The Conversation website also analyse the percentage of Australians identifying as non-heterosexual — that is identifying as other than a woman or man. Based on one survey they put the figure at 3.9 per cent for women and 2.9 per cent for men.

In addition to dramatically overstating the percentage of younger and older Australians who are other than heterosexual, the LGBTIQ+ material endorsed by Safe Schools mistakenly argues that sexuality and gender are fluid and limitless and that 'what you label yourself is up to you'.

Even though sexuality is a biological fact as at birth you are either a girl (XX) or a boy(XY) the *OMG I'm Queer* booklet tells students 'sexuality can't really be defined' and that 'sexuality is fluid and changes over time'.

Another booklet tells schools the person 'who understands most about their gender transition or affirmation is the student themselves' and that a student can be considered a 'mature minor and able to make decisions without parental consent'.

Ignored is that many children and students suffer from gender dysphoria. A condition the American College of Pediatricians describes as 'a psychological condition in which children experience a marked incongruence between their experienced gender and the gender associated with their biological sex'.

And the hypocrisy is that while LGBTIQ+ activists argue against treating children for gender dysphoria at the same time they are doing all in their power to convince vulnerable children that a procedure as extreme as gender transitioning is their right and that there are no harmful consequences.

As a result it should not surprise that in Sydney and Melbourne there has been a dramatic increase in children and teenagers presenting at gender clinics in our major public hospitals.

Not only does such a procedure ignore the reality that one's biological sex can never be changed, it ignores the fact that adolescence often involves feelings of uncertainty and doubt about one's sexuality.

As argued by Sydney's Professor Patrick Parkinson, it is wrong to assume that what a person feels is true during adolescence is fixed. He argues 'the evidence of volatility in terms of sexual attraction in adolescents is very strong indeed, across multiple studies.

No amount of cultural-left gender theory can ignore the fact as argued by the American College of Pediatricians that 'human sexuality is an objective biological trait'.

Even worse, as argued by the Vatican paper, gender theory ignores and corrupts the inherent, God given 'difference and reciprocity in nature of a man and a woman'.

Religious freedom: can the PM stay true to his word?

The Catholic Weekly
20 August 2019

Much of the debate centred around religious freedom defines the issue in terms of whether or not religious organisations like schools should be exempt from anti-discrimination acts. The assumption is that freedom of religion is just one among many other competing rights including freedom of expression and the freedom not to be unfairly discriminated against in relation to employment.

The American law professor Gerard Bradley who recently visited Australia as a guest of the Australian Catholic University's PM Glynn Institute argues otherwise. At a talk at the Melbourne campus of the ACU Bradley argues instead of subsuming religious freedom it should be treated as a distinct and irreducible good.

Based on natural law and the inherently moral and spiritual truth evidenced by religious faith Bradley, as does Sydney's Archbishop Fisher, argues religious freedom should be treated as a positive right essential to human flourishing.

While secular critics argue all citizens must abide by civil laws mandated by government those committed to Christianity and the teachings of the Church believe their duty to abide by God's law is higher and more absolute.

To hold a religious belief goes to the very core of what it means to be a free person and to compromise or restrict such a belief threatens the very nature of what it means to live in a liberal and open society.

As noted by Professor Bradley the belief religious freedom is paramount runs against the prevailing secular ideology that treats all truths as subjective and relative to the individual. Except, of course, with issues the cultural-left treats as beyond dispute like same-sex marriage and the right to undergo gender transition.

Based on the argument that the freedom to hold and express religious beliefs is an inherent right and not simply a privilege granted by the state it's clear that a number of consequences follow.

The first is that it is wrong to treat religious freedom as simply one freedom among many others. As argued by Larry Siedentop in *Inventing the Individual* Christianity and the New Testament are primarily responsible for the concept that each person has inalienable rights such as life and liberty.

The admonition 'There is neither Jew nor Greek, there is neither bond nor free, there is neither male nor female: for ye are all one in Christ Jesus' and the belief each person is made in the image of God underpins and informs the West's political and legal systems.

Christianity explains why in Medieval England the cleric and jurist Henry de Bracton was able to argue 'the king shall be under God and the law, for the law makes him king'.

Secondly, governments should always acknowledge and respect the right Christians have to remain true to their faith when designing and implementing any laws or requirements that contradict religious beliefs.

Christian doctors, nurses and health professionals should never be made to take part in practices like abortion and state sanctioned suicide. Penalising doctors for refusing to recommend a patient who wants to have an abortion or commit suicide is also a grievous injury to their religious faith.

While not directly involved, the reality is if a person facilitates such procedures he or she is implicitly involved and morally culpable. Religious bodies like schools also have the right to employ only those who share their uniquely religious character.

Not only because it is vital that all employed, both teaching and non-teaching staff, abide by the religious ethos and teachings of such schools; equally as important is a staff member acting as a good mentor and example to students.

Thirdly, the right to religious freedom involves the right to publicly express and enact such religious beliefs without being penalised or punished,

Contrary to secular critics who want to banish religion from the public square Professor Bradley argues religious freedom involves the right to enact and express such beliefs and teachings in public and in private life.

Whether arguing against same-sex marriage, gender fluidity and transgenderism, abortion or euthanasia Christians both have a moral duty to make public the Church's teachings as well as an inherent right to express their views without vilification and condemnation.

During the recent federal election campaign Prime Minister Scott Morrison, in a letter to Christian Schools Australia, wrote 'I believe there is no more fundamental right than the right to decide what you believe, or do not believe. That means Australians of faith should be free to hold and practise that faith without fear or discrimination against them'.

The Prime Minister also wrote 'My government believes that religious institutions must be free to uphold and to teach the tenets of their faith. Provided the teachings or practices of a religious institution do not contravene criminal law, the government has no business meddling with them'. One hopes the Prime Minister remains true to his word.

Secular critics get their man in Pell

The Australian
22 August 2019

It's a black day for the Catholic Church and an even worse day for Cardinal Pell whose appeal has been denied and who has been returned to prison to serve the remainder of his sentence as a convicted paedophile.

And while the victims of sexual abuse including the complainant will no doubt welcome and celebrate the result given the dissenting opinion of Judge Weinberg the suspicion still exists that justice may not have been fully served.

The sum total of the evidence used to convict Cardinal Pell relies on the evidence of one complainant who argued he and another choir boy had been sexually abused in 1996 by Cardinal Pell — who had only recently been appointed as Archbishop.

According to the lone survivor (the other boy who never reported being abused either to the police or his mother had subsequently died) the offenses occurred in the cathedral's sacristy after Pell had officiated at a Solemn Mass and weeks later in one of the cathedral's corridors.

Nothing will alter the fact that two of the judges rejected all of the 13 grounds for appeal put by Cardinal Pell's lawyers but there is also the reality that Justice Mark Weinberg, who is an expert in criminal law, concluded the convictions should not stand.

As noted by Chief Justice Anne Ferguson in his dissenting opinion Justice Mark Weinberg argued 'at times the complainant was inclined to embellish aspects of his account' and that 'his evidence contained discrepancies, displayed inadequacies and otherwise lacked probity value so as to cause him (Justice Weinberg) to have a doubt as to the applicant's guilt'.

And while the prosecution relied on the evidence of only one person, that is the surviving choir boy accusing Cardinal Pell, Justice Weinberg concludes there were credible witnesses arguing the alleged crimes had not been committed.

Justice Weinberg notes 'There was a significant body of cogent and in some cases impressive evidence suggesting that the complainant's account was in a realistic sense impossible to accept' and there was 'a significant possibility that the Cardinal may not have committed the offenses'.

Evidence presented raising doubts about the complainant's recollection of events included: the sacristy was usually inaccessible except for church officials and celebrants; the recently appointed Archbishop Pell after the end of the service normally thanked parishioners as they left; Pell was always escorted by at least one other church official and his robes made it physically impossible for him to commit the acts for which he was convicted.

As noted by Father Francis Burns who has been a celebrant at the cathedral for over 20 years 'the likelihood of anyone, young or old, wandering into the sacristy area during a ceremony and finding alter wine is, from my experience, non-existent. As is the likelihood of the Archbishop ambling about unaccompanied after Mass'.

Such was the questionable nature of the evidence presented by complainant in the first and second trials that the crime reporter and author John Silvester also casts doubt on the Pell's conviction. In *The Age* newspaper Silvester writes 'Pell was found guilty beyond reasonable doubt on the uncorroborated evidence of one witness, without forensic evidence, a pattern of behavior or a confession'.

In addition to the doubts raised by witnesses and those familiar with the layout of the cathedral and how Sunday masses are organised and managed there is also the concern that in relation to the legal process Cardinal Pell has had to endure the well has been truly poisoned.

For years secular critics have waged a concerted and pervasive campaign against Cardinal Pell and the Catholic Church. While there is no doubt the Church has been guilty of failing to protect children and failing to expose and punish those priests guilty it's also true the Catholic Church and Cardinal Pell have been the victims of a series of vitriolic and hostile attacks.

David Marr, for example, in a YouTube video describes Pell as a 'hard man (who) demanded obediency with the embodiment of the conservative churchman who was going to maintain the glory of his Church'. In a comment piece written for *The Guardian* Marr denigrates Pell for being intransigent, dogmatic and brutal.

Such have been the intensity of the attacks on Cardinal Pell that Chief Judge Kidd in the second trial and in his sentencing remarks acknowledged Pell had been 'publicly vilified' and described what occurred outside the court as 'a witch-hunt' promoting a 'lynch mob mentality'.

One of the tenets underlying our legal system is that not only must justice be done; it must also be seen to be done. Given the dissenting decision by Judge Weinberg there will always be the suspicion that in Cardinal Pell's case justice may not have been done.

Sorry is just not enough

The Daily Telegraph
2 October 2019

If ever there was an example of the cultural-left's hypocrisy and double standards go no further than Israel Folau and Kyle Sandilands. Folau has been vilified, attacked and condemned in the media and on social networking sites for arguing unless they repent drunks, adulterers, homosexuals, liars, thieves and fornicators would suffer in hell.

For expressing a sincerely held religious belief Folau has been sacked by Rugby Australia, lost millions in potential earnings and forced to take costly legal action to defend his reputation and, hopefully, restart his career.

Compare this to the response to a series of deeply offensive comments by Kyle Sandilands on KIIS FM over a week ago. When talking about the Virgin Mary, obviously a figure central to both the Christian and Islamic faiths as the mother of Jesus the Christ, Sandilands said Mary was not a virgin.

Instead of respecting the religious narrative surrounding the Annunciation and the virgin birth Sandilands joked someone had 'chock-a-blocked her behind the camel shed' and anyone who believed otherwise was talking 'bull sh*t' as a well as being as 'dumb as dog sh*t'.

One can only imagine the furore and backlash if Sandiland's disparaging and insulting comments had related to LGBTIQ+ people, people of colour or the Swedish climate activist Greta Thunberg. The self-righteous trolls in the Twittersphere would be in overdrive.

And while the sportswear company ASICS stopped sponsoring Folau and Alan Joyce, the CEO of Qantas, described Folau's comments as 'terrible for a large element of the community' the silence in response to Sandiland's comments about the Virgin Mary have been deafening.

Clearly, such is the power and influence of politically correct ideology and group think that if you espouse a religious belief it's open season and you are fair game. Vilify and insult religious beliefs for no good reason and you get a free pass and there are no consequences or sanctions.

To date, unlike Alan Jones who is another victim of corporate hypocrisy and virtue signalling, no sponsors have publicly withdrawn support and there has been no move to take Sandilands off air. And it's not as though Sandilands doesn't have form when it comes to making gratuitously offensive and insulting remarks.

Sandilands once abused the News journalist Alison Stephenson after she made some adverse comments about his TV show. Sandilands stated 'You're a bullshit artist, girl. You should be fired from your job. Your hair's very '90s. And your blouse. You haven't got that much titty to be having that low cut a blouse. Watch your mouth or I'll hunt you down'.

Even more disturbing than Sandiland's comments and the hypocrisy of the politically correct brigade is the reality that religion, especially Christianity and Catholicism, is increasingly under attack.

Some years ago the painting Piss Christ was exhibited in Melbourne; a painting that depicted the crucified Jesus apparently covered in urine. More recently, in Hobart as part of the Dark Mofo festival an inverted cross was displayed with little regard for the significance of the cross to Christians.

In Melbourne over the last four years, three Catholic churches have been the victims of arson attacks and in response to one of the churches being reduced to rubble the Australian actress Rachel Griffith stated she was 'quite elated'.

While it is understandable why so many are angry about the evil scourge of child-abuse that has plagued Catholic, Anglican and other Christian churches as well as secular organisations there is no excuse for insulting and demeaning one of the cornerstones of Australian culture and society.

Over 12 million Australians are Christian and religious schools enrol approximately 34% of students across Australia. Christianity underpins our legal and political systems and concepts like liberty, freedom of conscience, social justice and a commitment to the common good derive from the New Testament and Christ's teachings.

And Sandilands in his belated apology where he tries to excuse himself only digs the hole deeper. Rather than expressing sincere regret and remorse Sandilands excuses himself by saying it was only a joke and his intention was only to make people laugh.

Such an excuse displays an appalling ignorance and insensitivity to the central importance of religious faith and the fact that millions of Australians venerate the Virgin Mary as the mother of the one true Messiah who suffered and died for their redemption and salvation.

Proven by Andrew Bolt being penalised by the Human Rights Commission for offending Aboriginal Australians and Hobart's Archbishop Julian Porteous being made to answer to the Anti-Discrimination Commissioner for circulating a booklet opposing same-sex marriage it's obvious that there are two approaches to freedom of speech.

While it is OK to vilify and insult religion, especially Christianity, make the mistake of criticising or insulting those the cultural-left identifies as protected and you suffer adverse consequences.

Bruising our religion

The Daily Telegraph
24 December 2019

Anti-faith advocates portray Australia as a secular society under threat from a noisy religious minority, but in fact our nation is built on a set of beliefs that protect us all.

There's no doubt religious freedom is under attack by the extreme secular left and that more needs to be done to protect religious organisations and individuals from being attacked and vilified because of their beliefs.

And it's not just about Israel Folau or Margaret Court. The good news is, however, that the majority of Australians agree that protecting religious freedom is important. A survey carried out by Sydney's Centre for Independent Studies found that 78 per cent of those surveyed believed 'respecting religion is important in a multicultural society'.

The majority also agreed 'religious perspectives should be permitted in public debates even when others find them offensive'. Last week's release of the second draft of the commonwealth government's 'Religious Discrimination Bill 2019' is also positive news.

Central to the proposed Bill is the government's intention to legislate 'to eliminate, so far as possible, discrimination against persons on the grounds of religious belief or activity in a range of areas of public life'.

The government's legislation goes a long way to fulfill the promise made by Prime Minister Scott Morrison during the last election when he argued 'there is no more fundamental right than the right to decide what you believe, or do not believe. That means Australians of faith should be free to hold and practise that faith without fear of discrimination against them'.

As well as protecting religious freedom the Bill, under certain circumstances, also allows religious bodies and organisations to discriminate in relation to who they employ and the services they offer. Catholic schools, for example, will not be guilty of discrimination if they preference hiring teachers committed to the Catholic faith.

Health professional, including doctors, nurses, midwives, psychologists and pharmacists, while not being fully protected, will have the right to refuse being involved in any procedure that is contrary to their religious convictions and beliefs.

Not surprisingly, there are secular critics who argue against religious freedom and who are critical of the government's 'Religious Discrimination Bill'. *The Sydney Morning Herald's* Wendy Squires, a self-proclaimed atheist, argues the Scott Morrison government in supporting religious freedom is guilty of undermining 'the very tenets of our democracy'.

Squires argues 'According to our constitution, Australia is a secular society — one in which particular religious beliefs should not dictate or influence law'. The left leaning Public Interest Advocacy Centre also argues the government's 'Religious Discrimination Bill' is flawed and misconceived.

In a media release the Centre argues the Bill 'remains a threat to human rights' on the basis that religious bodies 'are given an almost free licenses to discriminate against people who do not share their religious beliefs'.

Drawing on identity politics, and without providing any evidence, the victim groups supposedly under threat include: 'women, lesbian, gay, bisexual, transgender and intersex people, people with disability and others exposed to derogatory comments in the workplace, schools and hospitals'.

What critics like Squires ignores is that while Australia is a secular society, to the extent that there is a division between church and state, the reality is that Australia's legal and political systems can only be fully understood in the context of Christianity and the New Testament.

That's why those responsible for writing Australia's Constitution when the colonies federated in 1901 included the words 'Humbly relying on the blessing of Almighty God' in the Preamble. And it's no accident that parliaments around Australia begin with the Lord's Prayer.

Concepts like the inherent dignity of the person and the right to life, liberty and the pursuit of happiness draw on Christ's teachings that all are made in the likeness of God. As stated in the Bible 'There is neither Jew nor Greek, there is neither bond nor free, there is neither male nor female: for ye are all one in Christ Jesus'.

As Christmas approaches it's timely to remember that approximately 52% of Australians identify as Christian and the birth of Christ represents one of the most momentous and significant events in the history of mankind. Only through God becoming man and offering redemption and forgiveness is it possible for Christians to find eternal salvation.

Christmas, as noted by Pope Benedict XVI , is a time when 'we contemplate the face of God, which is not revealed through force or power, but in weakness and the fragile constitution of a child. This "Divine Child" … demonstrates the faithfulness and tenderness of the boundless love with which God surrounds each of us. For this reason we rejoice at Christmas, reliving the same experience as the shepherds of Bethlehem'.

Cardinal's critics still having a hard time with the truth

The Catholic Weekly
13 April 2020

If ever additional evidence was required of the hostility and antagonism directed against the Catholic Church and Cardinal Pell as one of the Church's most articulate and persuasive advocates look no further than a number of the responses to the High Court's decision to free His Eminence from prison.

The High Court's unanimous decision by seven of the nation's most respected, experienced and eminent legal minds to overturn the Victorian Court of Appeal's dismissal of Cardinal Pell's appeal last year could not be more cogent and convincing.

Rather than accepting the 2–1 Victorian Court's decision the High Court judges conclude 'their Honours' analysis failed to engage with the question of whether there remained a reasonable possibility that the offending had not taken place, such that there ought to have been a reasonable doubt as to the applicant's guilt'.

More specifically, rather than accepting the complainant's allegation that the Cardinal had committed the offences the High Court found the jury that convicted His Eminence 'acting rationally (ought) to have entertained a reasonable doubt as to the applicant's guilt in relation to the offences involved in both alleged incidents'.

Such was the jury's failure to properly weigh all the evidence the seven High Court judges agreed there was 'a significant possibility that an innocent man had been convicted' and as a result 'ordered that the convictions be quashed and that verdicts of acquittal be entered in their place'.

One of the central tenets of Australian criminal law as argued by the Australian Catholic University's Vice-Chancellor Greg Craven in *The Australian* newspaper is that for a conviction to be recorded the offence must be proven 'beyond reasonable doubt'. As widely believed by many in the legal fraternity and I wrote last year in *The Australian* the sad truth is that Cardinal Pell was convicted unfairly and an innocent man was imprisoned for alleged crimes never committed.

Unfortunately, instead of accepting the High Court's unanimous decision given the prevalence of what the American academic Patrick Sookhdeo describes as Christianophobia many have refused to accept there was a mistrial and that Cardinal Pell deserves to be exonerated.

Clementine Ford, a feminist and one-time columnist with *The Sydney Morning Herald* and *The Age*, provides the most egregious and vile example when twitting she doesn't care what the High Court decides and that 'I hope George Pell has been sufficiently weakened by the prison he deserved to spend the rest of his miserable life in and he now dies slowly and painfully from COVID- 19'.

While the comments by Jon Faine, a former presenter on ABC Radio Melbourne, are no-where near as offensive or obnoxious, he also refuses to accept the decision by the highest court in the land. Faine condemns the decision by arguing it 'will send shivers through the entire Australian criminal justice system'.

According to Faine the High Court's argument that it's essential in relation to criminal cases to prove 'beyond reasonable doubt' carries no weight. Faine describes the High Court's decision as 'bizarre' and guilty of giving hope 'to anyone who has been convicted by a jury'.

David Marr, a long-time critic of Cardinal Pell also questions the validity of the High Court's decision when suggesting the court's judgement to free Cardinal Pell is a 'mighty triumph' not for the legal process but 'for the narrative of prejudice the church has spun all these years since the Melbourne police came for the cardinal in Rome'.

Instead of interpreting the High Court's decision as a vindication of our legal system where there are checks and balances and those who believe they are wrongly convicted can seek redress Marr argues it reinforces the narrative of 'The church being pursued by abuse victims, police and journalists with axes to grind'.

Marr also argues 'the court's decision reinforces scepticism in senior legal circles about prosecution of sex crimes committed a long time ago' and suggests the decision represents a 'crushing' blow for the young man who alleged he was sexually assaulted when a choir boy.

Ignored is that the young man concerned, known as witness 'J', stated after His Eminence had been freed 'I respect the decision of the High Court. I respect the outcome' and 'I understand their view that there was not enough evidence to satisfy the court beyond all reasonable doubt that the offending occurred'.

What both Faine and Marr also ignore, as noted by Viv Waller the lawyer representing 'J', is that the criminal justice system is obviously working without hinderance or restraint given the unforgivable high number of priests and clergy convicted by the courts for sexual offences.

Writing on The Conversation website two legal academics, Ben Matthews and Mark Thomas also argue the High Court's decision 'may undermine the confidence in the legal system, especially in child sexual prosecutions'.

Instead of accepting the fact that the High Court is the final court of appeal and that it has the right to judge decisions reached in lower courts the two academics describe its judgement as 'extraordinary' and 'strange justice indeed'.

Even worse, instead of Cardinal Pell being exonerated the academics expect further attacks when suggesting 'Pell has won today on a legal technicality, but he will continue to be assailed by multiple lawsuits'.

In an attempt to undermine the validity of the High Court's decision to free Cardinal Pell the two legal academics go on to argue 'In contrast, the complainant has been believed by a jury, by a majority judgement and by a substantial body of public opinion'.

The reactions to the decision to overturn Cardinal Pell's convictions, in addition to illustrating hostility to the Catholic Church, can only be described as hypocritical and biased. Many of those now so vocal in their condemnation of the High Court last year eagerly celebrated our legal system when it produced a result more suited to their anti-Christian, ideological convictions.

Political correctness and the distortion of language

The Catholic Weekly
10 July 2020

One of the most successful strategies used by the cultural-left to radically reshape society in its utopian image is redefining language to suit its agenda. As noted by George Orwell 'if thought corrupts language, language can also corrupt thought'; allowing words to be altered to enforce politically correct group think.

The word gay is an obvious example as activists have long since changed the meaning from being happy and carefree to describing homosexual men. Such has been the gay lobby's success that when Australian school children sing the song 'Kookaburra sits on the old gumtree' the line 'Gay your life must be' is altered to 'Fun your life must be'.

Rainbow provides another example where the word and the symbol have long been co-opted by the cultural-left to refer to a broad range of environmental, neo-Marxist and LGBTIQ+ activists grouped under the heading 'Rainbow Alliance'.

The way the word 'gender' has been redefined represents one of the more egregious examples of language control. According to The Shorter Oxford English Dictionary the word is a grammatical term used to denote whether 'nouns are masculine, feminine or neuter according as the objects they denote are male, female or of neither sex'.

Based on the research carried out by the psychologist John Money while at John Hopkins University during the 1950s the word was radically redefined to refer to an individual's sexual identity. Instead of biology and God's law determining whether a person was female or male Money introduced the description gender on the basis sexuality was a fluid and dynamic social construct.

Money's obituary in *The New York Times* describes this ground-breaking research as follows 'He was the first scientist to provide a language to describe the psychological dimensions of human sexual identity: no such language had existed before'.

Such has been the success of transgender activists in their campaign to normalise gender dysphoria that instead of chromosomes determining a person's sexuality the prevailing orthodoxy is that there is nothing fixed or absolute.

The Safe Schools Coalition booklet 'All of Us', made available to Australian schools and found on the Commonwealth Government's Student Wellbeing Hub, defines 'sexual diversity as a continuum' and tells students gender identity 'does not necessarily relate to the sex a person is assigned at birth'.

The booklet 'Safe Schools do Better', after erroneously arguing 15.7 per cent students are same sex attracted, intersex or gender diverse or trans when the figure is closer to approximately 5 per cent, suggests a 'person may identify as neither male nor female, or as both'.

As highlighted in George Orwell's novel *1984* language determines how we think and act and controlling language is a key strategy employed by totalitarian regimes to manipulate people and enforce groupthink. In Orwell's dystopian novel what is described as Newspeak leads to a situation where 'thoughtcrime' is impossible as 'there will be no words in which to express it'.

The slogan 'War is Peace, Freedom is Slavery, Ignorance is Strength' best illustrates how Big Brother subjugates citizens by radically altering the meaning of words and, as a result, controlling their ability to think rationally and independently.

Such is the insidious evil of distorting language and imposing group think Orwell writes 'The implied objective of this line of thought is a nightmare world in which the Leader, or some ruling clique, controls not only the future but the past ... If he says that two and two are five — well, two and two are five. This prospect frightens me much more than bombs'.

Australian universities and government bureaucracies instead of defending rationality and reason have long since become champions of cultural-left language control and group think. University Diversity Toolkits tell staff to use gender neutral pronouns, to describe the early convict settlement as an invasion and that it is wrong to describe pre-European Aboriginal culture as primitive.

The Victorian Department of Health and Human Services organises 'They days' where staff are told gender specific nouns like man and woman or pronouns like she and he are heteronormative, homophobic and transphobic.

While the cultural-left's use of politically correct language is widespread and now dominates public and private discourse in English speaking nations in particular there is nothing new in using language to persuade and convince.

What is described as rhetoric has been evident since the time of the ancient Greek philosophers and sophists and includes devices such as using emotive language and euphemisms and shifting the meaning of words to suit one's purpose and win the debate.

Where the cultural-left's use of language is dangerous and insidious is that it is calculated to dominate and control and to overthrow what is seen as an unjust, inequitable Western society riven with white supremacism, structural racism, sexism and transphobia.

And anyone who disagrees is condemned and vilified as Eurocentric, misogynist, heteronormative, xenophobic and worst of all Christian. So much for reasoned debate.

It's time to hear a prophetic warning

The Catholic Weekly
6 November 2020

As a result of cancel culture, the imposition of politically correct language and mind control and the destructive influence of the Marxist inspired Black Lives Matter movement the liberties and freedoms too easily taken for granted are constantly under attack and, if not already lost, are in danger of being eroded even further.

Karl Popper's *The Open Society and Enemies* first published in 1945 should be compulsory reading for those concerned about the existential dangers faced by democracy represented by the cultural-left's long march through the institutions.

While there's no doubt the culture wars beginning with the emergence of critical theory associated with Germany's Frankfurt School in the 1920s and the rise of postmodernism during the 1970s is of immediate concern Popper makes the point the conflict between tyranny and freedom 'is just as old or just as young as our civilisation itself'.

After differentiating between a tribal or closed society characterised by a submission to magical forces and an open society based on rationality and reason Popper warns the danger to liberty and freedom represented by totalitarianism is ever present.

Popper also argues, in opposition to those describing Western societies as riven with structural racism, white supremacism and class and gender inequality, ours is 'the best society which has come into existence during the course of human history'.

While acknowledging its flaws and injustices Popper describes Western civilisation as one 'aiming at humanness and reasonableness, at equality and freedom' and one in danger of being 'betrayed by many of the intellectual leaders of mankind'. Otherwise known as Lenin's 'useful idiots'.

One only has to compare the West's record of promoting liberty and freedom to Stalin's Russia where millions were starved and imprisoned and Mao's reign of terror plus Pol Pot's killing fields to realise the truth of Popper's thesis.

It was also the West that led the campaign to abolish slavery, that enacted a political system based on the sovereignty of the people and a legal system that protects citizens against unwarranted and unjustified government intervention and control.

Quite rightly, Popper concludes Marxist inspired regimes 'while promising paradise on earth never produced anything but hell'. Popper also justifies his preference for liberalism by arguing 'freedom is more important than equality; that the attempt to realize equality endangers freedom; and that, if freedom is lost, there will not even be equality among the unfree'.

Central to Popper's dismissal of 'utopian social engineering' associated with totalitarian ideologies is his critique of historicism. Described as 'the doctrine that history is controlled by specific historical or evolutionary laws whose discovery would enable us to prophesy the destiny of man'.

History tells us the Marxist belief in the inevitable collapse of capitalism and the arrival of a worker's paradise epitomised by the slogan 'from each according to his ability, to each according to his needs' has no basis in reality.

Similarly, the belief that all society needs to progress is centralised planning where the state dominates the market and there is no room for private ownership and entrepreneurship has also proven a dismal failure.

One of the most dangerous aspects of cultural-left ideologies including the deep green movement and radical gender, sexuality and post-colonial theories is the unflinching conviction their beliefs are beyond doubt and beyond criticism.

The causal link between carbon fuels and global warming as well as Greta Thunberg's belief the world will soon end if governments don't immediately ban fossil fuels and embrace renewable, carbon free energy, notwithstanding the science, is accepted as true and beyond reproach.

Notwithstanding the biological evidence that the overwhelming majority of babies are born as girls or boys hospitals now 'assign' gender at birth on the basis sexuality is a social construct and gender is fluid and dynamic based on one's preference.

Those committed to critical race theory and decolonising the curriculum are convinced Western civilisation offers nothing beneficial and that even Western science is merely one approach that has no right to be considered superior.

Ignored is that Western science based on rationality and reason as opposed to superstition and witchcraft represents a far more credible and effective way of analysing and evaluating truth claims and more closely approximating what constitutes the nature of things.

As noted by Popper, the conviction history can be manipulated and controlled by those convinced of their own infallibility inevitably leads to 'a doctrine of power, of subordination and submission'. Equally, if reason and rationality are rejected in favour of ideology and cant then liberty is lost.

Such is the poisonous impact of totalitarianism Popper warns 'if we are not prepared to defend a tolerant society, then the tolerant will be destroyed, and tolerance with them. We should therefore claim, in the name of tolerance, the right not to tolerate the intolerant'.

How dare these hypocrites 'culturally appropriate' Christianity

The Conservative Woman
2 February 2021

Considered a grievous crime by woke activists cultural appropriation involves copying, taking and in some cases exploiting things from a culture that is not your own. White, heterosexual, privileged men and women are always targeted on the basis they are the products of a capitalist society riven with structural sexism, racism and heteronormativity.

Peter Sellers playing the part of an accident prone Indian in the film *The Party*, Laurence Olivier in his role in Shakespeare's *Othello* and Prime Minister Trudeau of Canada blackfacing are all guilty of the crime.

Other examples of cultural appropriation include the cis female Scarlett Johansson planning to play the part of a transgender character and a white comedian at a Melbourne Comedy Festival whose act involved dressing as a geisha girl.

Such is the restrictive and doctrinaire nature of cancel culture that we now have a situation where white authors can never empathise with and write about non-whites, European fashion houses can never draw on tribal cultures for inspiration and during Halloween children can only wear politically correct costumes.

Woke activists even argue Western philosophy and science are derivative and guilty of stealing concepts and ideas from long since departed Islamic and African thinkers and scholars. Academics at the University of Sheffield argue Western science is guilty of 'whiteness and Eurocentrism' as it is was a major contributor to 'European imperialism'.

Nothing reveals the cultural-left's hypocrisy and double standards more than its condemnation of anyone considered guilty of cultural appropriation while, at the same time, ignoring and failing to punish any on the Left who commit the same offence.

One recent example involves a Canadian film that transforms Handel's oratorio Messiah to make it politically correct and ideologically sound. Drawing on the Bible's portrayal of the birth and life of Jesus including his eventual crucifixion and ascension into heaven Handel's *Messiah* is considered sacrosanct by Christians.

It's story of death and resurrection remains central to the Christian faith as it signals God's eternal love and the possibility of forgiveness and redemption. Instead of remaining true to what Handel composed woke activists have transformed the Messiah into a litany of politically correct vignettes.

As described by Dan Bilefsky in *The Age* (23 December 2020) the singers involved include a 'gay Chinese-Canadian tenor' wearing stiletto heels, a 'Tunisian-Canadian mezzo-soprano (who) reimagines Jesus as a Muslim woman wearing a headscarf' and an 'Indigenous singer' singing in her native language describing the 'snow covered landscape'.

Those responsible for politicising the *Messiah* justify their actions by arguing the revamped version centres on 'the rights of black people and other minorities' as well as providing the opportunity for the Indigenous performers to 'decolonise' themselves.

An even more egregious and reprehensible example of cultural appropriation involving Christianity is Apple TV's popular dystopian series *See* where the future is one where all are inflicted by blindness.

In one R 18+ graphic scene the actress playing the role of a demented, dictatorial queen pleasures herself while reciting a bastardised version of the Lord's Prayer including lines such as 'Give us this day your power', 'Condemn those who trespass against us' and 'For thine is the darkness, The power and the glory, For ever and Ever, Amen'.

Instead of offering God's forgiveness and redemption and promoting Christian love and charity the corrupted version of the Lord's Prayer is twisted to embody darkness and evil. A prayer to grant a tyrant Queen even more power to dominate and oppress others.

The above two examples are not isolated. Some years back the Melbourne based National Gallery of Victoria displayed Andres Serrano's *Piss Christ* that depicted a crucifixion submerged in a jar of urine. As argued by the then Melbourne Archbishop, George Pell, displaying the so-called work of art was deeply offensive and an example of blasphemy.

The annual Sydney Gay and Lesbian Mardi Gras provides yet another example of the cultural-left endorsing cultural appropriation as long as it targets those considered ripe for mockery.

Each year one of the apparent highlights of the LGBTIQ+ festival involves the Sisters of the Order of Perpetual Indulgence in a sacrilegious role play where gay/lesbian activists dress as nuns distributing blessings and indulgences to the Mardi Gras participants and audience.

That Christianity is targeted by the cultural-left and those who vilify and mock religion should not surprise. The origin of cancel culture and political correctness can be traced to Germany's Frankfurt School established in the 1920s by a number of neo-Marxist academics.

As noted by the Italian academic Augusto Del Noce, a central tenet of neo-Marxism is historical materialism that imposes a radical, secular view of history. An ideology by its very nature that persecutes religion and denies a spiritual and transcendent view of life and the life hereafter.

Christianity is the rock on which Australia stands

The Conservative Woman
12 May 2021

As argued by Sydney's Catholic Archbishop, Anthony Fisher, 'absolutist secularism' is an ever-present danger to Australian society as those hostile to the Catholic Church seek to banish Christianity from the public square and enforce a godless view of society.

Examples include Tony Abbott, when health minister, being attacked as the mad monk for questioning the increasing prevalence of abortion and Kevin Andrews, the federal member for Menzies, being vilified as a Christian for stopping the legislation to allow euthanasia in the Australian Capital Territory and Northern Territory in 1996.

The most recent example of prejudice and dislike directed at any politician brave enough to make public their religious convictions involves Prime Minister Scott Morrison who, at a recent national Christian Churches conference, made public examples of his faith.

The PM, while agreeing social media has its 'virtues and values', argued it was also a weapon that could 'be used by the evil one and we need to call that out'. One only needs to note the way social networking sites are used to dehumanise, exploit and manipulate people to realise the truth of such a statement.

Morrison also told those attending the conference that when he met people who had suffered because of natural disasters, he often prayed to alleviate their suffering and admitted that in embracing victims he was also 'laying hands on people'.

For admitting his faith and sharing his religious convictions it should not surprise that, like Israel Folau and Margaret Court for opposing homosexuality and same-sex marriage, the Prime Minister has also been criticised and attacked.

The Sydney social commentator and author Jane Caro's response on her Twitter account reads: 'Theocracies are very dangerous, particularly for women, the LBGTQI community and anyone who does not accept the dominant religion.' For expressing such a view, Caro adds that she will most likely 'be visited by the witch finder any day now'.

While not as extreme, the leader of the federal opposition, Anthony Albanese, also criticises the Prime Minister for expressing his religious beliefs. Albanese suggests 'the idea that God is on any politician's side is no more respectful than the idea that when somebody's sporting team wins, it's because of divine intervention'.

The Australian Labour Party leader also states that 'the separation between Church and state are (sic) important — implying religion, in this case Christianity — is a strictly private affair that has no place or role in Western, liberal democracies such as Australia.

The ABC commentator Stan Grant puts a similar case when arguing 'we are not the United States', where it's expected presidents are religious.

Contrary to what Caro argues, the reality is that Australia never has been and, in all likelihood never will be — despite the PM's religious faith — a theocracy like Islamic Iran and Saudi Arabia.

Under the Australian constitution, there is a clear division between Church and state and holding a religious office is not a prerequisite for being a member of parliament.

While such is the case, and to that extent we are a secular society, it is also wrong to argue Christianity is insignificant and that it has no role to play in the nation's political and legal systems. As argued by the Perth academic Augusto Zimmerman in *The Christian Foundations of the Common Law*, religion underpins and informs the nation's parliaments and courts.

Zimmerman writes: 'When considered alongside the development of colonial laws, the adoption of the English common law tradition and American system of federation, it is evident that the foundations of the Australian nation, and its laws, have discernible Christian-philosophical roots.'

Concepts such as the inherent dignity of the person, the right to liberty and freedom and the need to commit to social justice and the common good, as detailed in *Inventing the Individual The Origins of Western Liberalism* by Larry Siedentop, have their origins in Christ's teaching detailed in the New Testament.

Those arguing there is no place for Christianity in public life, especially politics and government, also ignore the reality that whether individuals are aware of it or not, every decision they make is informed and influenced by a particular philosophy or belief system.

Cultural-Left activists committed to banishing religion from the public square are often motivated by neo-Marxist ideology; one where Karl Marx and Friedrich Engels are the prophets, the Communist Manifesto is the bible and those committed to the faith are promised a socialist utopia on this earth.

As such, it is hypocritical and illogical to argue that socialist ALP members of parliament and Green politicians worshipping the Gaia have the right to decide public policy according to their beliefs while denying Christians the same right.

Reciting the Lord's Prayer Important

The Age
3 August 2021

The dominant religion in Australia is Christianity and central to Christianity is the Lord's Prayer. This explains why both the national and the Victorian parliamentary sessions begin with the words 'Our Father, which art in heaven: Hallowed be Thy Name'.

Largely ignored in the current debate about the place of the Lord's Prayer is that both parliaments also include a Welcome to Country in acknowledgement that Aborigines lived in this land for thousands of years long before the arrival of the First Fleet in 1788.

Given the Victorian Parliament respects Aboriginal history, culture and spirituality it's only fair and reasonable the same privilege is granted to citizens whose ancestry can be traced to the United Kingdom, Ireland and Europe who have settled this land.

In relation to ancestry the 2016 national census notes 89.9 per cent of those surveyed identified as Australian, English, Irish and Scottish with Europeans representing six of the top 10 ancestries. The equivalent figure for Aborigines is 2.8 per cent.

And while there is no doubt the percentage of Australians identifying as Christian has diminished since the time of federation according to the 2016 census 'Christianity is once again the dominant religion in Australia, with 12 million people, and 86 per cent of religious Australians, identifying as Christians'.

The argument the Victorian Parliament must continue to include the Lord's Prayer is strengthened by the fact we have inherited a Westminster parliamentary form of government and a common law system heavily influenced by the Bible.

As argued by the Perth-based legal academic Augusto Zimmermann in 'Constituting a Christian Commonwealth: Christian Foundations of Australia's Constitutionalism' in *The Western Australian Jurist*, the freedoms we take for granted as a Western liberal democracy are based on Christian concepts including the inherent dignity of the person and a commitment to social justice and the common good.

Zimmermann argues 'It can, at the very least, be said that Judeo-Christian values were so embedded in Australia so as to necessitate the recognition of God in the nation's founding document'.

Larry Siedentop in *Inventing the Individual The Origins of Western Liberalism* makes the same point when detailing how our political and legal institutions and way of life are underpinned and nourished by Judeo-Christianity.

The Bible's admonition 'There is neither Jew nor Greek, there is neither bond nor free, there is neither male nor female: for ye are all one in Christ Jesus' represents a revolutionary call for equity and social justice for all.

As detailed in the Australian Catholic University's PM Glynn Institute booklet 'Amen: A history of prayers in Parliament' the significance and the power of the Lord's Prayer cannot be overestimated.

The prayer, recognised by all Christian churches and traditions, has 'a special significance for Christians as a prayer Jesus himself prayed and which encourages us to approach God in the familiar or intimate terms of father'.

The words of the Lord's Prayer are deeply profound and important; especially for politicians who have the responsibility to act morally and in the best interest of those they represent and the wider community they are dedicated to serve.

In the Machiavellian political world of machinations and subterfuge reciting a prayer provides a moment of reflection and meditation. The opening words 'Our Father' makes the point there is a higher authority that members of parliament should recognise as they are not the ultimate source of wisdom and truth.

The words 'And forgive us our trespasses, as we forgive them that trespass against us' reminds members of parliament that they are only human and fallible and as suggested by the English poet Alexander Pope 'To err is human, forgive divine'.

The line 'Lead us not into temptation but deliver us from evil' reinforces the danger of hubris and the conceit that as members of parliament they are immune from temptation and sin. The prayer also recognises there is evil in the world and that the role of government is to promote truth, justice and the common good.

The Victorian government led by Premier Daniel Andrews is leading Australia in terms of recognising the value and significance of Aboriginal history, culture and spirituality represented by the need for truth-telling about Victoria's past.

While it is a right and proper thing to do it would be disingenuous not show Victoria's Christian community the same respect. It is also wrong to ignore the history and traditions underpinning the unique form of government we have inherited.

As argued by Melbourne's Archbishop the Most Reverend Peter Comensoli, the Lord's Prayer embodies 'a significant legacy of faith that has contributed to our democracy, and its institutions, that ought to be honoured and respected'.

Liberty demands the state respect religion

Spectator Australia Flat White
1 October 2021

While the Commonwealth Government is yet to table the revised version of its Freedom of Religion Bill there's no doubt religions are under attack across Australia and the Victorian government, in particular, no longer supports freedom of religion and the right religious bodies have to manage their own affairs.

The recent decision by the Victorian government to mandate only fully vaccinated worshipers can attend religious services is a direct attack on people of faith not wanting to be vaccinated. Unlike the New South Wales government that is willing to remove restrictions by early December, there is no such commitment from Daniel Andrews.

The Victorian Government's decision to legislate to deny religious schools control over who they employ further illustrates how religious freedom is being undermined. Such a law will force faith-based schools to employ staff whose beliefs and actions are inimical to the religious tenets such schools embody.

Banning religious priests, imams and rabbis from counselling against gay conversions involving puberty blockers and radical surgery represents yet another example of how Andrews seeks to impose extreme secular ideology on people of faith.

And the Victorian government is not alone given the decision by the NSW Property Minister, Melinda Pavey, to renege on a previous agreement stopping the government from taking control of cemetery trusts managed by the Catholic Metropolitan Cemeteries Trust.

Sydney's Catholic Archbishop Anthony Fisher, who was involved in the previous negotiations carried out by the NSW Deputy Premier John Barilaro, describes the government's actions as 'betrayal of our trust in your good faith'.

Employment and the ability to publicly express one's beliefs is another area where religion is under attack. While Israel Folau being banished from the Wallabies is the most obvious example of someone suffering because of their beliefs, such discrimination is increasingly common.

In his chapter in *Cancel Culture and the Left's Long March* John Steenhof details how a number of other Christian rugby players felt intimidated because of what happened to Folau. Such was the unease in the rugby camp Sekope Kepu describes how the prayer meetings he was involved in came to an end.

Such is the extent to which religious views are being stifled and the risk of losing employment or being publicly vilified Steenhof concludes 'Australian laws are being weaponised to silence religious voices and to cancel religious Australians who express ideas'.

At a time, according to a survey commissioned by the Australian Christian Lobby, when 64% of those surveyed agreed it was wrong to discriminate against religion it's time governments respected and supported religious freedom. Especially when international agreements enshrine freedom of religious belief and freedom to worship free of government coercion and control.

The International Covenant on Political and Legal Rights, along with race, sex, colour, language, states governments do not have the right to discriminate based on religion. Article 18 specifically mandates 'freedom of religion' and Australia ratified the International Covenant in 1980.

Australia has also ratified the *United Nations Declaration on the*

Elimination of All Forms of Intolerance and of Discrimination Based on Religion or Belief that states freedom of religion is 'one of the fundamental elements' of a person's 'conception of life and that freedom of religion or belief should be fully respected and guaranteed'.

While it's obvious more needs to be done to protect religious freedom even more concerning is the growing opposition to the commonwealth's Religious Freedom Bill currently being finalised by Attorney-General Michaelia Cash. Unlike the American Constitution's First Amendment that protects religious freedom, the Australian Constitution does not make such a commitment.

To address this shortcoming the Religious Freedom Bill 'prohibits discrimination on the ground of religious belief or activity in key areas of public life'. The bill's explanatory notes state 'All people are entitled not to be discriminated against on the basis of their religious belief or activities in public life and are entitled to the equal and effective protection of the law'.

Such is the antipathy towards religion that even those who should protect freedom of speech and equality before the law, like the LINO politicians Trent Zimmerman, Dave Sharma and Tim Wilson, want the bill watered down so religious organisations like schools will not be protected.

It's ironic that at the very time cultural-left activists argue against discrimination and governments advocate the rights of disadvantaged groups like gays those of religious faith are targeted and their freedoms restricted.

Western liberal democracies like Australia are based on political and legal rights where religious organisations and individuals must be respected and treated fairly and justly. When governments, for whatever reason, abridge and deny such rights we are on the road to serfdom where the state reigns supreme.

About the Author

Since first warning about the dangers of political correctness during the mid-1990s Dr Donnelly has established a reputation as one of Australia's leading conservative commentators and authors fighting against politically correct group think and language control that are undermining Western societies and stifling free and open debate. In opposition to neo-Marxist inspired critical theory and absolutist secularism Kevin champions the strengths and benefits of Western civilisation and the contribution and on-going debt owed to Judeo-Christianity.

Kevin writes regularly for *The Daily Telegraph, The Herald Sun, The Australian, Spectator Australia, Quadrant, The Catholic Weekly* and the London based *The Conservative Woman*. Kevin also appears regularly on Sky News and is often interviewed on 2GB, 5AA and ABC Radio National. He is the author of *How Political Correctness is Destroying Australia, How Political Correctness is Destroying Education, How Political Correctness is Still Destroying Australia, A Politically Correct Dictionary and Guide* and is the editor of *Cancel Culture and the Left's Long March*.

Kevin is a Senior Research Fellow at the Australian Catholic University and in 2016 was made a Member of the Order of Australia for services to education.

Contact Kevin Donnelly

kevindonnelly.com.au

kevind@netspace.net.au

kevin.donnelly.1023

ESIaustralia